JOHN DEWEY:
Master Educator

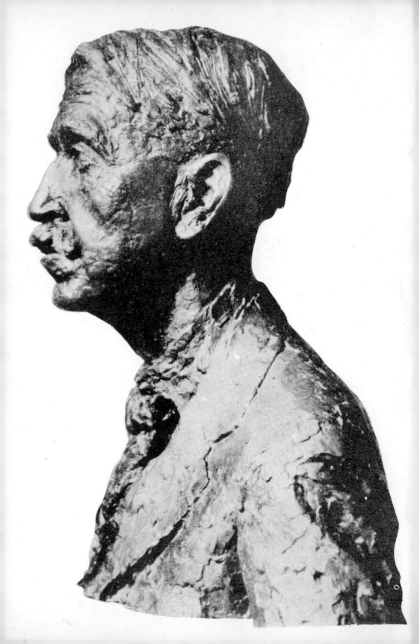

JOHN DEWEY:

Master Educator

Edited by

WILLIAM W. BRICKMAN

Editor, School and Society
Professor of Education, New York University

and

STANLEY LEHRER

Vice-President and Managing Editor
School and Society

New York, 1959
Society for the Advancement of Education

For

SYLVIA BRICKMAN

and

LAUREL LEHRER

Preface

IF THE CURRENT SCARCITY of new books about
John Dewey is any indication, interest in the
master educator appears to be on the wane. Even
now, on the occasion of the 100th anniversary
of Dewey's birth, too few publishers have decided
to grant posterity in print to him. Actually, the
importance of Dewey's contributions to education has not diminished in the minds of educators. This book recognizes his ageless significance,
his impact in America and abroad.

The book has developed from material that
the editors first presented in a special issue of
School and Society, Oct. 10, 1959, commemorat-
ing the Dewey centennial. This material is supplemented by other information.

Junius L. Meriam, who remembers Dewey and
reminds us that he "lives on in history," exem-
plified the spirit of the book's whole undertaking
by working on the necessary data—despite a long
and serious illness—and not holding up publication. To all contributors go the editors' thanks
for invaluable co-operation.

WILLIAM W. BRICKMAN
STANLEY LEHRER

New York City,
October , 1959

Introduction

During 1959, intellectuals in various parts of the world are observing the 100th anniversary of the birth of one of the best-known thinkers of the present century, one of the most influential educators, and one of the most modest of modern men—John Dewey. This commemoration comes at a time when the name of Dewey has been dragged in the mud by those who, although unfamiliar with his ideas, had no hesitation in attributing the worst faults of education to him. It is fitting and proper to talk and write about Dewey if for no other reason than to demonstrate the depth of his enemies' ignorance.

Let it be said once and for all that Dewey himself opposed an either-or position. He did not demand uncompromising agreement, as some of his followers have done. Criticism of Dewey's doctrines did not mean loss of the master's favor. Anyone finding fault with Dewey is worthy of listening to if he bases his critique on Dewey's thinking rather than on fantasy. One need not be an admirer of Dewey to respect the man and to recognize his influence in this country and in many foreign lands.

The very fact that foreign books, some of impressive length, continue to be written about Dewey is an indication that there is a universal interest in his work and ideas. The blind, unknowing enemies of Dewey, if they showed but a modicum of objectivity and fairness, would not have stooped to near-gutter language in disposing of the person. They might take a lesson from educators in other parts of the world, who, while not fully agreeing with Dewey, acknowledge the usefulness of his thought and practice.

John Dewey may not have been the world's greatest educational philosopher, but he was a pedagogue who inspired widespread rethinking of educational objectives, principles, and procedures. Because the inspiration was and continues to be universal, it is appropriate to honor him 100 years after his birth.

WILLIAM W. BRICKMAN

Contents

JOHN DEWEY:
Master Educator

John Dewey's Life and Work in Outline

By WILLIAM W. BRICKMAN

THE BIOGRAPHICAL DATA concerning John Dewey are not available in concise and reasonably complete form. The following represents an attempt at such a list.

Oct. 20, 1859—Birth of John Dewey on a farm near Burlington, Vt. Son of Archibald Sprague Dewey (1812-91), a grocer, and Lucina Rich Dewey (born 1830). Younger brother of Davis Rich Dewey, later a distinguished economist. The Deweys were derived from the Huguenot family, Douai, which migrated to Kent, England, in the second half of the 16th century.[1] The first to reach America, Thomas Duee, who changed his name to Dewey, settled in Dorchester, Mass., in 1634. He is the ancestor of Admiral George Dewey, former Governor Thomas E. Dewey, and Dr. John Dewey.

The year 1859 saw the publication of Charles Darwin's "Origin of Species," Herbert Spencer's "What Knowledge Is of Most Worth?," Alexander Bain's "Emotion and the Will," Karl Marx's "Critique of Political Economy," John Stuart Mill's "On Liberty"; the deaths of Horace Mann and Alexander von Humboldt; the birth of Pierre Curie, Pierre Janet, Ludwig Zamenhof, Edmund Husserl, Henri Bergson, Sholom Aleichem, and Berthhold Otto; the passage of the Casati Law in Italy; the founding of Cooper Union; the founding of the Massachusetts Institute of Technology; and John Brown's Raid (Oct. 16-18).

1875—Graduation from high school.

1875-79—Attendance at the University of Vermont. Davis and John were the first college students in the Dewey family, which was descended from Thomas Dewey who had settled in Massachusetts during the 1630's. They were able to attend college because of its nearness, low tuition, and some scholarship help.

1879—B.A., Phi Beta Kappa.

---

[1] Possibly from the de Wei ("of the Meadow") family from Flanders via England.

1879-81—Teacher of Latin, algebra, and natural science, high school, South Oil City, Pa.

1881-82 (winter)—Teacher in village school, Charlotte, Vt. Studied history of philosophy with Prof. H. A. P. Torrey of the University of Vermont.

1882—Publication of his first writings in the *Journal of Speculative Philosophy,* edited by William Torrey Harris: "The Metaphysical Assumptions of Materialism" (April) and "The Pantheism of Spinoza" (July). Two more articles were published by Dewey in this journal: "Knowledge and Relativity of Feeling" (Jan., 1883) and "Kant and Philosophic Method" (April, 1884). Dewey's first article was abstracted in the *Revue Philosophique* (Jan., 1883). This is the earliest foreign mention of John Dewey.

1882-84—Graduate work at the Johns Hopkins University. Taught undergraduate course in the history of philosophy, spring semester, 1883. Fellowship, 1883-84.

1884—Ph.D. The dissertation, "The Psychology of Kant," never was published and "no copy is owned by the university" (M. H. Thomas).

1884-88—Instructor and assistant professor of philosophy, University of Michigan. Marriage to Alice Chipman (1886). First article on education, "Education and the Health of Women," *Science* (Oct. 16, 1885). First published book, "Psychology" (New York: Harper, 1886). "Leibniz's New Essays Concerning the Human Understanding" (1888). "The Ethics of Democracy" (1888).

1888-89—Professor of philosophy, University of Minnesota.

1889—First book on education, "Applied Psychology: An Introduction to the Principles and Practice of Education," by J. A. McLellan and John Dewey (Boston: Educational Publishing Co.).

1889-94—Chairman, Department of Philosophy, University of Michigan.

1893—First article on education below college level, "Teaching Ethics in the High School," *Educational Review* (Nov.).

1894-1904—Chairman, Department of Philosophy, Psychology, and Pedagogy, University of Chicago. Teaching of graduate courses.

1895—"The Psychology of Number and Its Applications to Methods of Teaching Arithmetic" by James A. McLellan and John Dewey (New York: Appleton). Published also in England (London: Edwin Arnold, 1895).

1896-1903—The Laboratory School of the University of Chicago. Described in "A Pedagogical Experiment," *Kindergarten Magazine* (June 1896); and in "The

University School," *University* (of Chicago) *Record*, I (Nov. 6, 1896, pp. 417-419).

1896—"Interest as Related to Will."

1897—"My Pedagogic Creed." "Ethical Principles Underlying Education."

1899—"The School and Society." Published also in England (London: P. S. King & Son, 1900).

1899-1900—President, American Psychological Association.

1900—Editor, *The Elementary School Record*, a series of nine monographs.

1902—"The Child and the Curriculum." "The Educational Situation."

1902-1904—Director, School of Education, University of Chicago.

1903—"Studies in Logical Theory" (with seven others).

1904—LL.D., University of Wisconsin.

1904-30—Professor of philosophy, Columbia University.

1905-06—President, American Philosophical Society.

1908—"Ethics," by John Dewey and James H. Tufts.

1909—"Moral Principles in Education."

1910—LL.D., University of Vermont. "How We Think." "The Influence of Darwin on Philosophy."

1913—"Interest and Effort in Education." LL.D., University of Michigan.

1915—Founder and first president, American Association of University Professors. "German Philosophy and Politics." "The School and Society" (revised edition). "Schools of Tomorrow" (with Evelyn Dewey). LL.D., Johns Hopkins University.

1916—Charter member, first teacher's union, New York City. "Democracy and Education." "Essays in Experimental Logic."

1917—LL.D., Illinois College.

1919—Lectures at Tokyo Imperial University (Feb.-March).

1919-21—Lectures at the National Universities of Peking and Nanking.

1920—"Reconstruction in Philosophy" (Tokyo lectures). "Letters from China and Japan" (with Alice C. Dewey). LL.D., Peking National University.

1921—Editor, "The Alexander-Dewey Arithmetic," by Georgia Alexander (three volumes).

1922—"Human Nature and Conduct."

1924—Study of educational conditions in Turkey.

1925—"Experience and Nature."

1926—Study of educational conditions in Mexico.

1927—Death of Mrs. Alice Chipman Dewey. "The Public and Its Problems."

1928—Study of educational conditions in Soviet Russia.

1929—"Characters and Events," two volumes of Dewey's essays under the editorship of Joseph Ratner. "Impressions of Soviet Russia and the Revolutionary

World, Mexico-China-Turkey." "The Quest for Certainty." "The Sources of a Science of Education" (with six others). President, People's Lobby. National chairman, League for Independent Political Action. Gifford lectures, University of Edinburgh. LL.D., Columbia University.

1930—LL.D., University of Paris. "Individualism Old and New."

1930-39—Professor emeritus of philosophy in residence, Columbia University.

1931—"Philosophy and Civilization." "The Way Out of Educational Confusion."

1932—Revised edition of "Ethics," by John Dewey and James H. Tufts. LL.D., Harvard University.

1933—Revised edition of "How We Think."

1934—"Art as Experience." "A Common Faith."

1935—"Liberalism and Social Action."

1937—Chairman, Commission on Inquiry into the Charges Made Against Leon Trotsky in the Moscow Trials. "The Case of Leon Trotsky," report of hearings by John Dewey, *et al.*

1938—"Logic: The Theory of Inquiry." "Experience and Education." "Not Guilty," the report by the Inquiry Commission on Trotsky (John Dewey, *et al.*).

1939—"Freedom and Culture." "Theory of Valuation."

1941—"The Bertrand Russell Case" (edited with Horace M. Kallen).

1946—"Problems of Men." Marriage to Mrs. Roberta L. Grant (Dec. 11). Adopted children—John Dewey, Jr., and Adrienne Dewey. Ph.D. (Hon.), University of Oslo. D.Sc., University of Pennsylvania.

1949—"Knowing and the Known" (with Arthur F. Bentley).

June 1, 1952—Death of John Dewey, New York City.

Biographical Information

Jane M. Dewey, "Biography of John Dewey," pp. 3-45, in Paul A. Schilpp, editor, "The Philosophy of John Dewey." Evanston: Northwestern University, 1939.

John Dewey, "From Absolutism to Experimentalism," pp. 13-27, in George P. Adams and William Pepperell Montague, editors, "Contemporary American Philosophy," Vol. II. London: Allen and Unwin, 1930. An intellectual autobiography.

Selections from Dewey's Works

Joseph Ratner, editor, "The Philosophy of John Dewey." New York: Holt, 1928.

Joseph Ratner, editor, "Intelligence in the Modern World: John Dewey's Philosophy." New York: Modern Library, 1939.

A. H. Johnson, editor, "The Wit and Wisdom of John Dewey." Boston: Beacon, 1949.

Irwin Edman, editor, "John Dewey: His Contribution to the American Tradition." New York: Bobbs-Merrill, 1955.

Birthday Anniversary Volumes

"Essays in Honor of John Dewey on the Occasion of His Seventieth Birthday." New York: Holt, 1929.

"John Dewey: The Man and His Philosophy." Cambridge: Harvard University Press, 1930.

Paul A. Schilpp, editor, "The Philosophy of John Dewey." Evanston: Northwestern University, 1939 (pp. 611-676, bibliography).

Sidney Ratner, editor, "The Philosopher of the Common Man: Essays in Honor of John Dewey to Celebrate His Eightieth Birthday." New York: Putnam, 1940.

Kenneth D. Benne and William O. Stanley, editors, "Essays for John Dewey's Ninetieth Birthday." Urbana: University of Illinois, 1950.

Bibliography of Dewey's Writings

Milton H. Thomas, "A Bibliography of John Dewey: 1882-1939." New York: Columbia University Press, 1939.

Reminiscences of Dewey and His Influence

By WILLIAM HEARD KILPATRICK

My first personal contact with Prof. Dewey was in an 1898 summer course in education at the University of Chicago. However, I got little from the course; I was not ready for its thinking and I was not accustomed to Dewey's method of teaching. His practice, as I later learned, was to come to the class with a problem on his mind and sit before the class thinking out loud as he sought to bring creative thinking to bear on his problem.

A monograph by Dewey, "Interest as Related to Will," which I studied two years later under Charles DeGarmo, did have a deep and lasting effect on me and on my thinking. In it Dewey was analyzing a controversy as to the relative educative effect of "interest" and "effort" upon a pupil. The "interest" proponents had perverted the Herbartian doctrine of "interest" into a superficial "sugar-coating" device of "making things interesting"; the "effort" side, led by William T. Harris, charged that such "sugar-coating" would spoil children and was wrong anyway. What was needed was the building of character, and effort was essential to accomplishing this. To secure effort they proposed to coerce children into effort, by threats and punishment when necessary.

Dewey said, in effect, you are both wrong; by sugar-coating you cannot make things effectively interesting; and coerced effort—forcing children to go through motions without putting themselves into what they do—will fail to build character. Especially you have misunderstood the inherent relation between interest and effort; typically, personally felt interest is the first stage of an on-going experience in which correlative personal effort is the effecting stage. Thus, proper interest and proper effort cannot be opposed; they are, in essence, correlative, the one leading to and demanding the other.

At that time, I was a college professor of mathematics, but for several years I had been indulging in education as a side interest. This Cornell experience of Dewey, with its new insight into the educative process as character-building, persuaded me to give up mathematics and center my interest henceforth on education as my life-work. For various good reasons I could not act on my change of interest until 1907, when I received a scholarship to Teachers College, Columbia. Prof. Dewey was then teaching philosophy at Columbia; and for the next three years I took all his courses, having decided meanwhile to major in philosophy of education.

I entered upon my 1907 work with Prof. Dewey thinking that in philosophy he still was a neo-Hegelian. For a time, Dewey—along with many others—had followed this neo-Hegelian line; and I, too, after working in philosophy at Johns Hopkins in 1895-96, had accepted it as my personal outlook. But now I found that Dewey, stressing the conceptions of process, the continuity of nature, and the method of inductive science, had built an entirely new philosophy, later called Experimentalism. As I worked with him during three constructive years, I gave up neo-Hegelianism and accepted instead the new viewpoint, thereby gaining a fresh and invigorating outlook in life and thought.

From that time until Prof. Dewey's death in 1952, I had great satisfaction in the many contacts with him. Dewey read and approved the manuscript of my 1912 book, "The Montessori System Examined." When he himself had finished seven chapters of "Democracy and Education," he turned these over to me for criticism and to suggest other topics for completing the book. I was then teaching a course in Principles of Education; so I made a list of philosophic problems that troubled me in this course and turned them over to Dewey. At first he rejected my list, but later he redefined a number of the problems and these now appear as chapters in the completed book.

Another instance of personal experience with Dewey came after he had retired from Columbia and I meanwhile had accumulated considerable experience in teaching philosophy of education. He was offered a post as visiting professor in philosophy of education. Though his reputation as a creative thinker in both philosophy and philosophy of education was unsurpassed, he felt unsure as to certain practical details of the new post and accordingly came to me for advice. That I was glad to help needs no words here.

As to the origin of Dewey's educational ideas, some thought he had derived these from Rousseau and Froebel. I once asked him about this and he told me explicitly that he had not read either one until after he had formed his educational outlook. He did say, in another connection, that he had got help in his educational thinking from Francis W. Parker, who was active in education in Chicago when Dewey came to the University of Chicago. As to the origin of Dewey's philosophy of life (and, consequently, of education), he himself makes it clear that he got his psychology from William James. This means, as Dewey later brought out, that he and James were both deeply indebted to Darwin's "Origin of Species." It seems probable that from this source Dewey derived the conceptions of process, continuity of nature, and the method of inductive science referred to earlier. It also seems that certain important elements in Dewey's outlook—his belief in equality—came from the creative frontier background which he shared in his Vermont family in common with so many other Americans.

As to Dewey's comparative place in the history of philosophy, I place him next to Plato and Aristotle. As to his place in the history of philosophy of education, he is, as I see it, the greatest the world has yet beheld. As to his current influence in education, I place him in company with William James, Francis W. Parker, and Edward L. Thorndike—those who most efficiently have helped to shape our existent American educational thinking.

John Dewey in History

By JUNIUS L. MERIAM

Lives of great men all remind us
We can make our lives sublime,
And, departing, leave behind us
Footprints on the sands of time.
—LONGFELLOW

A MAN of national, even international, reputation, John Dewey is known for his scholarly attainments, his insight into human society, his acquaintance with people's difficulties, his wisdom in finding ways to assist, and his disposition to serve three classes of people: the lay public, the teaching profession, and the children in our schools. Indeed, he was a man destined to be known in history.

Anyone who had the pleasure of meeting Dewey face to face was deeply impressed—by the quiet twinkle in his eye, an expression of joy in his readiness to serve adults in social and industrial life; by the humbleness in his countenance, an expression of readiness to render assistance to teachers in their profession; and by the firm grip of his handshake, an expression of determination to be a guide to school children in their development.

Reference was made above to three classes of people whom Dewey wished to help. A keynote throughout Dewey's many writings may be expressed in his own words: "Learning? Certainly, but living primarily, and learning through and in relation to this living" ("The School and Society," p. 53, 1899 edition). This means that the adult public needs to center its attention upon the inclusive philosophy of social life; that the teaching profession center its instruction of youth upon their manner of living; and that pupils in school look foremost to their own life activities. Living for these three classes of people is primary. Learning is a secondary matter, a means of serving the more important—that of living. Dewey rightly emphasizes: the child is already intensively active, and the question for both teachers and the lay public is that of taking hold of the activities and giving them direction.

The reader of Dewey's writings must accept that author primarily as a philosopher and secondarily as a school administrator. At first, he was an instructor and assistant professor of philosophy at the University of Michigan (1884-88); later, head of the department of philosophy and education (1894-1904), including a position as director of the School of Education (1902-04) at the University of Chicago; thereafter, professor of philosophy at Columbia University (1904-30), and then he became emeritus. Quite naturally, his major writings were in the field of philosophy and, in his case, with emphasis upon social philosophy.

Thus, as may be expected, the bulk of his writings was addressed to the adult public. It is sufficient here merely to glance at the nature and scope of his writings in this field. The titles of some writings are a key: "Psychology," "Psychology and Social Practice," "Moral Principles in Education," "How We Think," "Human Nature and Conduct," "Art as Experience," "Liberalism and Social Action," "Freedom and Culture," "Education and the Social Order."

A recent book, "John Dewey in Perspective," by George Geiger, a professor of philosophy, clearly emphasizes the over-all character of Dewey's writings. A few of the chapter titles readily present that "perspective": "The Affirmation of Experience"; "The Nature of Value"; "Inquiry, Knowing, and Truth"; and "Intelligence and Liberalism." Needless to say, Prof. Geiger sees in Dewey an interminable flow of social philosophy. He states in the preface to his book: "To correct the sometimes narrow and occasionally vulgar interpretation of his [Dewey's] philosophy there will be deliberate emphasis on the consummatory and esthetic aspects of Dewey's philosophy of experience."

It may be said that Dewey's early book on psychology (1887, when he was only 28 years of age) was based largely upon the extensive readings to which specific page references are made at the close of each chapter. For example, in his chapter of 53 pages on "Elements of Knowledge," Dewey refers to 78 sources, his readings in this field; and in his next chapter, "Processes of Knowledge," of 73 pages he cites 54 sources to which he refers. These writings are by American, British, French, German, and Italian authors. Dewey remarked: "The literature of the association of ideas is exceedingly voluminous," clearly evidenced by his own references. Thus, this first book of Dewey's and the many writings that follow indicate that he himself, as author, is voluminous in his writings. These mainly are addressed to social philosophy for the adult public.

One who reads Dewey is readily impressed by the glittering generalities in the social philosophy which he expounded. To quote a few statements as characteristic: "We may sum up the discussion in a few generalized statements." "Speaking generally the purpose is to facilitate our dealings. . . ." "The occasion of deliberation is confusion and uncertainty." "Popular opinion is little troubled by questions of logical consistency." Insofar as a writer (in this case, Dewey) deals in generalities, his statements are readily accepted. If specific items are presented, targets are open to attack. Dewey adroitly avoided exposure to this danger. Thus, in the main, Dewey won extensive approval of his sayings, his writings, and his social philosophy by reason of his generalizations. His popularity is a product of this character of his utterances. He avoided administrative details. With this touch of omission we must recognize a great quantity of high quality in Dewey's help given to public thought at large.

Turn next to the second class to which Dewey offered help—the profession of education. Here he wrote much less than in the field of social philosophy. Certain writings were addressed quite definitely to the profession, though always with considerable tinge of social philosophy.

"My Pedagogic Creed," by Dewey, is especially addressed to teachers. This was one of his early contributions (1897). In this creed, he makes 55 declarations, each opening with the words, "I believe . . ." Characteristic of all these statements is the second one: "I believe that the only true education comes through the stimulation of the child's powers by the demands of the social situation in which he finds himself." Dewey's series of beliefs closes with this high ideal: "I believe that in this way the teacher always is the prophet of the true God and the usherer in of the true kingdom of God." Thus, he continues his social philosophy.

In "The School and Society," the definite article "The" points somewhat to an institution other than social philosophy. Indicative for that whole volume is a statement in the first paragraph: "What the best and wisest parent wants for his own child, that must the community want for all of its children. Any other ideal for our schools is narrow and unlovely." Here Dewey does address the social public as well as the teaching profession. This book consists of four "talks" before teachers, parents, and others who showed interest in the school started by Dewey as an experiment within his social philosophy. He and those associated with him opened this school with questions and problems rather than with definite proposals for action. The school was said to be conducted as a form of home and community life. Therefore, living was the primary objective. Was it such? Immediately involved was the question: How to teach the conventional school subjects. Thus, "primary" became weakened. Here was an allied objective. In this school, under the influence of Dewey's social philosophy, living, as primary, served as a "vital motive" (his own words) for technical instruction in the traditional subjects—the Three R's. The *Elementary School Record* (a series of nine issues closing in Dec., 1900, with Dewey as editor) dealt with the traditional school subjects.

In these studies and writings by Dewey there is evidence of a duality—two objectives: living, recorded as primary, and technical learnings, considered as essentials. Dewey seems not to have held fast to living as the real objective, with learning as only a means to accomplish that fundamental purpose. This administrative deficiency seems to have led from philosophy and education at the University of Chicago to the chair of philosophy at Columbia University.

The third group of people to whom Dewey

was destined to render help is that of our pupils in school. And they do need his help. Quite naturally as professor of philosophy, Dewey addresses much less of his writings to this class of people, though with an implied emphasis through his philosophy. Thus, with rather deficient administrative direction of his school at the University of Chicago, Dewey leaves to his readers his invitation to "read between the lines."

While attending appreciatively and, indeed, with much admiration to Dewey's social philosophy, the general public assigns to him large responsibility for much of the adversely credited "progressive" education in our modern schools. This so-called "progressive" school is not unquestionably progressive, as is frequently claimed, and Dewey is censured as largely responsible. The truth is that the standards of Dewey's behavior are high. He calls for social behavior of a high order and for action that speaks louder than words. Admit a bit of inconsistency between his social philosophy and his advocacy of acquiring conventional school learnings, but believe wholeheartedly in his plea, "Learning? Certainly, but living primarily." Adverse criticism of Dewey, in relation to our modern education, is due to the failure by school officials to interpret and apply adequately his principles to practical problems in the conduct of our schools. Deficiency is not in Dewey as a philosopher but in school officials as administrators of his philosophy.

Let us briefly contrast Dewey's school—as viewed between the lines—with much that is practiced in our modern schools.

1. Dewey's school outmodes the traditional grade room, so rightly characterized as "self-con-

tained," one teacher for a group of pupils throughout the day. Dewey's is a living school building. Pupils work in a social studies room only half of the school day. Then they are in an assembly room for music, for dramatization of stories, folk dancing, social parties, motion pictures, etc. Pupils co-operate in handwork rooms, including kitchen and lunchroom. Pupils engage in physical activities in gymnasium and outdoor sports (not "recesses"). Pupils are thus in contact with several teachers each day.

2. Dewey's school is democratic though under guidance by teachers. Pupils are largely responsive to the group within which there is much interaction and co-operation. A pattern is found in community life.

3. Dewey's school operates through a longer school day; no recesses for needless relaxation and fewer vacations and no long ones in summer. Such is social life and industry.

4. Dewey's school discontinues the traditional school subjects *as such*. Living is primary, the one objective. Learning is secondary, a means to accomplish the great objective.

5. Dewey's school encourages in each pupil his greatest achievement possible. Examinations are not formal tests. The pupil grows and "passes" from year to year, from grade to grade. But this rests upon the spirit of serious application.

6. Discipline in Dewey's school is an exacting demand in that system itself, not the office of a teacher in charge. Respectful attitude replaces disregard.

7. Dewey's school provides wholesome play as an inherent portion of the program, not a recess for relaxation. Play for young children is co-ordinate with work, one phase in natural development.

8. In short, Dewey's school is one of wholesome living within the school regime in contrast to that of formal education of the traditional stamp. Dewey's school exemplifies his social philosophy—"Learning? Certainly, but living primarily."

The year 1959 marks the centennial of John Dewey's birth. Since centennial celebrations have been in vogue from the beginning of our Christian era and will continue as a habit among us humans, it may be appropriate to commemorate some centennial year of Dewey's great achievements. For example: In the year 1987, a psychology to equal that of Dewey's emphasis on activities; in the year 1997, a "pedagogic creed" to compare with that of Dewey's; in the year 2049, an experimental school fashioned to study "Education and the Social Order." By such achievements, John Dewey lives on in history.

Dewey and American Education, 1894-1920

By MAXINE GREENE

In 1894, John Dewey became chairman of the Department of Philosophy, Psychology, and Pedagogy at the University of Chicago; in 1916, he published "Democracy and Education," his definitive statement of educational belief. The decades in between represent the period of his growth as educator, psychologist, and educational philosopher. He published much in those years, lectured to many thousands of people in and out of his classrooms, and was active in numerous organizations. What were the effects of all this work at the time it was done? What was the actual response to John Dewey during those active and consistently productive years?

To answer this, it is necessary to determine the influence Dewey seems to have had upon educational theory and discussion and, too, to discover how his writing, teaching, and example affected practice in the public schools and in the "progressive" schools of the day.

The judgments of educational historians are summary, often contradictory; and they change with vantage point in time. Thomas Davidson, who knew Dewey, did not mention him in "A History of Education" (1900). A Kantian and a devotee of moral discipline, Davidson said conclusively that "the foundations of modern education for rational liberty were securely laid" by Herbart, Froebel, and Rosmini. Paul Monroe's "A Textbook of the History of Education" (1905), however, laid emphasis on Dewey's role in resolving the old conflict between individual and social tendencies in the schools. Dewey, Monroe affirmed, "has done more than anyone else to elaborate the eclectic view of education. . . ." Ellwood P. Cubberley, in "The History of Education" (1920), wrote that the work of the Dewey Laboratory School "was of fundamental importance in directing the reorganization of the work of the kindergarten along different and larger lines," and that it also was significant in redirecting teaching in social studies, art, and manual training. Eby and Arrowood, in "The Development of Modern Education" (1934), went further, saying that Dewey's experiment "produced phenomenal effects." Adolphe E. Meyer, in "The Development of Education in the Twentieth Century" (1939), asserted that Dewey's influence was not immediately felt to any significant extent.

It is best to turn to the man himself and to see him against the background of a changing America. He began his educational labors in a context of far-ranging inquiry and controversy on Herbartian and Froebelian theories, problems of method, child study, and the whole matter of the scientific approach to education. Judgments of his influence mean little if they derive from insufficient knowledge of what Dewey was trying to do *within* that context; and it is well to start with what he himself thought most significant in his work.

A common misconception has to do with the Laboratory School at the University of Chicago, a school too many think of as the archetype of a "progressive" school. The Laboratory School was established when Dewey was chairman of his tripartite department at Chicago and was directly related to the work being done in educational theory and psychology by his staff. More specifically, it was connected with "a body of philosophical and psychological conceptions," and its purpose was to test a particular philosophy of knowledge and conduct through practical application. In 1936, Dewey wrote that "the school by intention was an experimental school, not a practice school, nor (in its purpose) what is now called a progressive school." Its aim was "to deepen and broaden the range of social contact and intercourse, of cooperative living," and its experiments "were directed to the discovery of tendencies, powers, and needs which would lead to desirable social results."[1]

The school attracted much attention. Visitors came to see and were often horrified by what seemed to them to be a complete break with tradition. They brought, Dewey said, "the image of a convent school" and found activity which they interpreted as rampant individualism if they did not identify the social element as a new version of subordination to teacher and textbook. The Chicago newspapers reflected the hostility of such visitors and, on more than one occasion, objected violently to what was going on.

Nevertheless, the work of the school tended to increase attendance at Dewey's lectures in the classroom. Moreover, because of the peculiar status of the school and the need for voluntary financial backing, it was necessary for Dewey to participate in many public meetings, to join with educators and interested laymen in cam-

---

[1] K. C. Mayhew and A. C. Edwards, "The Dewey School," The Laboratory School of the University of Chicago, 1896-1903 (New York: Appleton-Century, 1936), J. Dewey, "Theory of the Chicago Experiment," Appendix II, p. 464.

paigns to muster support. The first edition of "The School and Society" (1899) was, in fact, a collection of Dewey's money-raising speeches, and an indication of its effect may be found in a book review in *The Dial* the next year. "When the first reports of the University Elementary School of Chicago reached the outside world," said the collaborating reviewers, "they were not taken seriously save by isolated persons here and there." Educators, they continued, did not think it would last long or teach any new lessons; but, to their surprise, "the school has lived on, is now in its fourth year, and has more eyes fixed on it today, undoubtedly, than any other elementary school in the country." The reason, it was held, could be found in "current dissatisfaction with our conventional common school education, and the desire to find something better."[2] Merle Curti was to describe that dissatisfaction as a discontent with the conservatism of William T. Harris;[3] and William Heard Kilpatrick was to write, "The bold daring of a school that could reject completely the ordinary course-of-study curriculum was bound to attract attention."[4] Henry Steele Commager has called "The School and Society" the most influential of Dewey's books and said that he "had already emerged as one of America's most original and profound thinkers" when it was published.[5] For all this, the reviews of the book were sparse. There was mention of it in the journal, *Education*, in 1899; it was reviewed without enthu-

---

[2] *The Dial*, 29:98, Aug. 16, 1900.

[3] M. Curti, "The Social Ideas of American Educators" (New York: Scribner, 1935).

[4] P. A. Schilpp, editor, "The Philosophy of John Dewey" (New York: Tudor, 1931), p. 460.

[5] H. S. Commager, "Living Ideas in America" (New York: Harper, 1951), p. 587.

siasm by W. S. Sutton in the *Educational Record* in 1900; it was referred to in the *Elementary School Teacher* (July, 1901) in a "Syllabus of Lectures and Lessons on Philosophy of Education"; and Charles A. McMurry quoted from it in "Elements of General Method" (1903). There is no evidence of widespread response in the nonprofessional magazines.

In Chicago, Dewey participated in many meetings with other educators of the Illinois Society for Child Study and the National Herbart Society. These conferences were as important as his public meetings in providing a channel through which his thought could reach the schools. Besides providing platforms, they extended the possibility of publication and ensured a receptive audience. "Interest as Related to Will" first appeared in the *Second Supplement to the Herbart Yearbook for 1895*; "Ethical Principles Underlying Education" was published in the *Third Yearbook* (1897). "Interest as Related to Will," now thought to be Dewey's earliest definitive educational statement, attracted some immediate attention; and its importance as a theoretical contribution was recognized in the *Educational Review* (Vol. 12, 1896) and in the *Public School Journal* (Vol. 15, 1895-96).

Perhaps of equal significance were Dewey's friendly and professional associations in Chicago. Ella Flagg Young, one of his good friends, was district superintendent of the Chicago schools during his early years at the university and a colleague of his for a time. She resigned her appointment when Dewey left and remained, as Jane Dewey writes, not only friendly with him, but influential in his thought.[6] When it is

---

[6] P. A. Schilpp, *op. cit.*, p. 29.

recalled that she was elected president of the NEA in 1911 and used her rich opportunities to speak in behalf of the "new education" for many years, her part in shaping a response to Dewey can be seen. The association with Jane Addams and Hull House played another role, although a less definable one. The settlement was a center for many kinds of people, among them artists and writers on the Chicago scene, and Dewey's contacts there were manifold. It must be noted, however, that there was no visible response to his work in artistic circles at the time.

There was, in addition, James R. Angell, who had studied with Dewey at Michigan (and with James and Royce at Harvard) and who became a colleague at Chicago. Angell, a psychologist, later became one of the most influential proponents of a functional psychology, a carrier of the thinking of James and Dewey conjoined.

Thorstein Veblen, professor of political economy, and Franz Boas, curator of anthropology in the Field Museum, also were at Chicago at the same time as Dewey. There was a well-known affinity between the thinking of the three as members of the "Chicago Group," and Morton White has pointed to the relationship between the emphasis upon the values of community life in "The School and Society" and in "The Theory of the Leisure Class," also published in 1899.[7] It may well be that Veblen played some part in the struggle to maintain the Laboratory School; but we must avoid an identification of the undoubtedly wide response to the "revolt against formalism" in philosophy, law, and economics with the response to Dewey's educational thought as such. The movement against

---

[7] M. White, "Social Thought in America" (Boston: Beacon, 1957), pp. 94-95.

abstraction and *a priori* thinking carried forward on historical, evolutionary, and functional grounds certainly involved Dewey as well as Veblen, Beard, Robinson, Holmes, and the rest. As a current of thought and action, it exerted a large and definable influence in American institutional life in the first decade of this century; and Dewey's role in it as ethical thinker and logician is generally recognized. This does not permit us to assume, however, that a direct influence on educational theory and practice was a necessary concomitant.

We may grant that the Laboratory School and the thinking associated with it were publicized, and that the effort to keep the school alive attracted many prominent individuals, but we must still ask whether any measurable influence was exerted on educational theory at the time. We ought to keep in mind that the school not only was an experimental school, but that the social phase was dominant in its curriculum. "We do not expect to have other schools literally imitate what we do," Dewey wrote. The school was concerned with demonstrating the feasibility of a principle. "Its task is the problem of viewing the education of the child in the light of the principles of mental activity and processes of growth made known by modern psychology."[8] This indicates that the school was not meant to prod others into experimentation, since, according to Dewey, "the purpose of performing an experiment is that other people need not experiment, at least not experiment so much, but may have something definite and positive to go by." The fact that few educators followed Dewey's lead in this regard is not, in

---

[8] "The School and Society" (Chicago: University of Chicago Press, 1915), p. 88.

itself, evidence of lack of influence. The question of whether the experiment done at Chicago provided something "definite and positive" for practicing schoolmen is more to the point.

Those who seriously attempt to characterize Dewey's contribution agree, in general, that his influence was exerted in the broadening of the curriculum, the correlating of subjects, the development of a less rigid notion of discipline, and the relating of school studies to their applications in life. It is worth noting, for example, that Dewey was involved in the discussions going on between 1895 and 1905 relative to the reorganization of instruction in the elementary and secondary schools. Cubberley points out that "a new direction" was given to the discussions in 1901 by Dewey and in 1902 by William Rainey Harper at meetings of high-school representatives at the University of Chicago.[9] Speaking at the NEA on the "Situation as Regards the Course of Study" (1901), Dewey pointed out the advantages of a six-year elementary school and highlighted a number of the problems involved in school reorganization to meet the social and industrial demands of the time. Much of what was done and said remained theoretical, but the possibility exists that, by defining some of the urgent questions, Dewey left his mark on the organization of curriculum in the schools.

"How We Think" was published in the *Elementary School Teacher* (Dec., 1903) and may be considered, at least in part, a consequence of the work done in the Laboratory School. It is well known that the Herbartian influence was dominant in American education from 1898 to 1910 and that the strict concern with the Five

---

[9] E. P. Cubberley, "History of Education," p. 551.

Steps, content, and character formation began to modify in the succeeding years. Kilpatrick writes that Herbartianism began to "fade away" after the publication of "How We Think," but it is difficult to establish a casual relation, especially when we recall such works as William C. Bagley's "The Educative Process" (1905), which represented a modification of Herbartianism hardly traceable to Dewey's works. It is likely, however, that, in the renewal of efforts to define principles of method, the problem-solving approach was taken into account. W. W. Charters, who had studied with Dewey, attempted to apply Dewey's theory in the context of subject-matter organization in his "Methods of Teaching" (1909); and George D. Strayer, in "A Brief Course in the Teaching Process" (1911), showed Dewey's influence in the stress he placed on the importance of presenting purposes and problems to the child. Edward L. Thorndike referred to Dewey when he talked of the relevance of the problem-attitude to motivation in his "Psychology of Learning" (1913).[10]

Nonetheless, a look at the *Addresses and Proceedings* of the NEA in the years immediately following Dewey's Chicago experiments shows us that his work impressed public-school teachers little, if at all. In 1907, for instance, William Arthur Clark, State Normal School, Kearny, Neb., spoke of the need for a "Pedagogical Laboratory in the Scientific Study of Education." In stressing the importance of research and suggesting that pedagogy was a science capable of study, he asserted, as if such a proposal never had been made before, that there *was* such a field as

[10] E. L. Thorndike, "Educational Psychology," Vol. II (New York: Teachers College, Columbia University, 1913), p. 225.

scientific study. He referred to Fechner and the psychologists but not to John Dewey. To sharpen the point, we might note that, in the same issue (p. 23), the only other mention of laboratory method was made by the superintendent of the Rochester public schools, who associated the method with Froebel and left it at that.

In the ensuing years, nothing of significance can be found in the NEA discussions with relation to the Chicago experiments. Beginning in 1911, Ella Flagg Young began to bring reports of experimentalism to the meetings; but, at first, there was little response. In 1913, Louise M. Alder, State Normal School, Emporia, Kan., spoke on the "Effect of the Scientific Spirit in Education on Kindergarten Relationship to Materials" and mentioned the "growing body of so-called 'progressive kindergartners' who were pioneers in this movement of reconstruction." This was part of the tendency to bring up criticisms of Froebelian mysticism before the kindergarten section between 1913 and 1915.[11] The activity idea, as systematized by Dewey, was reflected in those criticisms; but, as Wesley points out, there was no real concern for the needs of the individual pupil until 1915 and no application of scientific method in discussion of curriculum making until 1920.

As far as the social and ethical emphases in Dewey's work were concerned, there is no evidence that these exerted any marked effect on the thinking of public schoolmen during this period. Turning again to the NEA *Addresses and Proceedings*, we find a continuing emphasis on the "essentials" for their own sake, on democracy viewed as a spiritual enterprise, and on

[11] E. B. Wesley, "NEA: The First Hundred Years" (New York: Harper, 1957), p. 164.

the dangers of "extreme secularism" in the schools. In 1907, the president of Iowa State University, speaking on "Democracy and Education," said that democracy needed, above all, scholars who would be its spiritual guides. In 1908, M. G. Brumbaugh, superintendent of the Philadelphia schools, stressed the need for a "fund of common knowledge" for promoting the welfare of the state rather than the individual in the schools. Addressing the Committee on Moral Training, Brumbaugh described the "virtues of civilization" and defined morality as conscientiousness. This was typical of discussions on morality among schoolmen at the time.

Now and then there was some mention of "self-activity," of the child relating to the world. In 1911, John W. Carr, Bayonne superintendent, quoted Dewey on ethical principles; in 1916, Luella A. Palmer, assistant director of New York City kindergartens, quoted Dewey on the matter of morality learned in contact with actual situations; but, aside from the work of Ella Flagg Young, such responses were few. When Dewey himself spoke in 1916, he addressed the NEA on "Nationalizing Education" and put his prime stress on the use of education in the interest of national unity and for the promotion of "national" ideas.

In "Schools of Tomorrow" (1915), Dewey and his daughter did describe certain public school systems that were putting new theories into practice; but Dewey did not take credit as the progenitor of their work. Among the public schools mentioned were those in Gary, Indianapolis, and Chicago, and Dewey said that they showed fundamental resemblances "illustrating the direction educational reform is taking." There were tendencies, he wrote, towards more freedom and towards an identification of school life with social life; and many teachers were attempting to bring about the adjustment between children and their environment by means of "learning by doing" procedures. Implicit in the book, however, is a recognition that the changes occurring must be interpreted as functions of social change in its largest sense—urbanization, expanding technology, collectivity, population mobility, and all the other aspects of a growing industrial economy.

The random sample of schools studied did not suggest, of course, that major alterations were occurring in the majority of American schools. In 1902, at the memorial services for Col. Francis W. Parker, described in the *Elementary School Teacher,* Dewey sadly described Parker's efforts to make education a force in community life; and he commented, "He was a pioneer, and to many he seemed a faddist." It is entirely likely that Dewey was talking about himself as well as the deceased. Many commentators agree that he felt an enormous sense of futility in 1904, when he resigned from Chicago; and Harold Rugg, Adolph E. Meyer, Kilpatrick, and others feel that his influence was at a very low ebb in the next 10-15 years.

Parker's "practice school" for elementary teachers had been merged with the Laboratory School in the new Chicago School of Education, formerly Parker's Chicago Institute. The merger was arranged without Dewey's consultation, and it amounted to the abandonment of the Laboratory School.[12] No provision was made for the continuation of Dewey's experiments nor for the work of the teachers concerned with them;

[12] P. A. Schilpp, editor, "The Philosophy of John Dewey," p. 34.

and the supporters of the school, outraged, organized a Parent Teachers Association which tried to raise funds to guarantee the continuation of the work. Jane Dewey has written that "educators all over the country" sent letters of protest to the administration; but the president's indifference to the Laboratory School finally led to Dewey's resignation. Rugg comments, in reference to this period, "I am told by those who knew him well that he regarded his work in educational reconstruction of little avail."[13] The first appraisal he agreed to do of the Laboratory School came more than 30 years later in the chapter he wrote for "The Dewey School."

It is still commonly believed that, when Dewey left his work in educational reconstruction and turned to the rethinking of his philosophical position, his influence as educator was carried on by the "protest" schools which grew up in various parts of the country, especially after 1912. If we recall, however, the experimental nature of the Laboratory School, its psychological, philosophical, and social concerns, we can well understand Rugg's insistence that few of the "progressive" schools were traceable to Dewey's influence. For one thing, as Rugg and Ann Shumaker asserted, the only one that legitimately could be called experimental was the Lincoln School, established in 1917.[14] In "The Dewey School" (p. 420), it is said that the "most important issues of the Dewey School experiment are not used by the progressive schools as criteria, nor have they been supplemented by further experiment reported to a

---

[13] H. Rugg, "Foundations for American Education" (New York: World Book Co., 1947), p. 555.

[14] H. Rugg and A. Shumaker, "The Child-Centered School" (New York: World Book Co., 1928).

consulting central body." There was innovation, yes, but not directed and designed inquiry.

The "social phase" and the experimentalist ethic had equally little effect on the predominantly individualist protest schools. They characteristically responded to some of the psychological cues but seldom, if ever, adopted the Laboratory School's approach to problem-solving in the context of social experience. Margaret Naumburg went so far as to say in "The Child and the World" (1928) that, "as things stand today," only in the lower and kindergarten grades did training schools and model schools "attempt any serious readaptation of the curriculum to the psychological needs of the child."

It is not surprising that Dewey made his well-known statement in 1938 dissociating himself from the "progressive education" movement. Even the private protest schools discussed in "Schools of Tomorrow" could scarcely be classified as belonging to the Dewey tradition. The only really experimental school among them was the project initiated by Junius L. Meriam at the University of Missouri in 1904; but, although he was "undoubtedly influenced by Dewey," as I. B. Berkson said in "Education Faces the Future" (1943), his conception of education was quite different from Dewey's and primarily concerned with the fulfillment of needs at various stages of child growth. Most of the schools studied by the Deweys fell, as they pointed out, between the currents of spontaneity and the control of growth by means of the material presented; and few of them can be conceived as responses to what Dewey actually was saying.

Still, after 1910, his books gradually came into use in various teacher training institutions; and some attention was paid to him as "teacher of teachers" in the public press. One of the more revealing articles was written by Randolph Bourne for the *New Republic* (March 13, 1915). Commenting on the limited popular awareness of Dewey's achievement, Bourne wrote: "Pamphlets and reports of obscure educational societies, school journals, university monographs, and philosophic journals limited to the pedant few; these are the burial places of much of this intensely alive futuristic philosophy." He complained that the "Educational Creed . . . is still lost in an out-of-print cheap bulletin in some innocent series for elementary teachers," that "The School and Society" frightened people with its infantile cover, and that only some essays and "How We Think" had reached the public. "No man with such important things to say ever published in forms more ingeniously contrived to thwart the interest of the prospective public," Bourne went on, attributing this to Dewey's extravagant dread of show. His democracy "seems almost to take the extreme form of refusing to bring one's self to the attention of others," he concluded; and, if we add to this the ambiguity and obscurity of his writing, we can understand more easily why it was so difficult for Dewey to evoke a productive response to what he intended to say.

A rendering of his philosophic thought was included in the wave of "progressivism" that reached its peak in the 1912 elections and in Woodrow Wilson's "New Freedom." The progressive movement, as Gabriel and others point out, was closely related to philosophic pragmatism, perhaps because pragmatism, from the days of its Jamesian formulation, was a function of American activism and individualism. "The social planners of the Progressive Era turned for their philosophy to pragmatism. They put their faith in science." But then Gabriel added, ". . . sometimes a suspicion arises that the disciples of Progressivism, in an effort to appear modern, tricked their doctrines in the latest intellectual mode without fully understanding the implications of the doctrines of James and Dewey."[15] Much the same can be said about Progressivism as it affected the schools.

When "Democracy and Education" was published, it aroused little immediate response, and there were remarkably few reviews in the periodicals. This may have been due to the war situation, to the decline of the progressive idea in political life, and to the general resistance to a gospel of political liberalism wedded to educational experiment. E. E. Slosson did a sketch of Dewey as educator in the *Indianan* (March 6, 1917); Denton L. Geyer wrote on "The Wavering Aim of Education in Dewey's Educational Philosophy" in *Education* (April 1917), in which he complained of the absence of clearly defined goals in Dewey's point of view and of the fact that the conflict between "individual and socialist" was left unreconciled. Morris Raphael Cohen, in the *New Republic* (Sept. 2, 1916), commented that Dewey's contributions to ethics and education were "illustrations of his central theses" which mainly had to do with "how people think and how their thoughts become effective," but he asserted that "there are many indications that pragmatism may soon become the popular philosophy of our progressive democracy."

Most students agree that it took the creative advocacy of William H. Kilpatrick at Teachers

[15] R. H. Gabriel, "The Course of American Democratic Thought" (New York: Ronald, 1940), p. 336.

College and Boyd H. Bode at Ohio State University to communicate Dewey's theories of teaching, learning, and thinking in a way that could arouse a widespread practical response. Kilpatrick's "The Project Method" (1918) referred to Dewey in connection with the problem type of project[16]; but it is clear that, by then, the Deweyan approach was being reshaped to some extent in the light of Kilpatrick's own development and of further psychological inquiry and altered social demands.

It is difficult to see the Progressive Education Association, organized in 1919, as a specific response to Dewey's work, although many men versed in and committed to the experimentalist philosophy were involved. Its original statement, however, expressed commitment to "progress in education in all its forms" and, for all its implicit social concern, was concerned primarily with individual "natural development."

Even as Dewey's contribution must be seen in the context of contemporary thought and social change, so must the response to his achievement. Between 1894 and 1920, educators only could respond in terms of their prime concerns and discontents and in the framework of ongoing learnings they saw systematized in Dewey's work. His mode of expression was singularly prone to misinterpretation, and this encouraged existing tendencies to see in what he said that which seemed familiar or desirable.

Lawrence K. Frank, writing on Dewey's contributions to the study of culture and personality, has said: "The genesis of all new developments is in the critical, reflective, and creative thinking of the gifted individuals who are able

---

[16] *Teachers College Record*, 19:319-335, September 1918.

to free themselves, in part at least, from their coercive traditions and to make new assumptions and develop new methods and techniques of inquiry."[17] This may well be relevant to Dewey's educational work. It clearly took over 20 years for American educators in general to free themselves sufficiently to discover what Dewey actually said with regard to a philosophy of experience, the scientific method, the guidance of learning, the nature of democracy, and the social role of the schools.

[17] S. Hook, editor, "John Dewey: Philosopher of Science and Freedom" (New York: Dial, 1950), p. 88.

John Dewey as Teacher

By HAROLD A. LARRABEE

THERE MUST BE hundreds of persons living today who once enjoyed the inestimable privilege
of being numbered among the students of John
Dewey. It can safely be said of them, moreover,
that they have one thing in common: a total
inability to recognize, in the current journalistic
stereotype of Dewey as bogeyman and personal
devil bent upon ruining American education,
the modest, humane, intellectually humble Ver-
monter who was the ablest philosopher America
has yet produced. The inability or the disinclina-
tion (or both) to understand what Dewey tried
for 60 years or more to teach has spread over the
nation like a blight, even penetrating the White
House, to the point where someone has asserted,
to our shame, that "John Dewey could not be
elected a member of any school board today in
the United States."

Not that such a fate is anything unusual for
a seminal and disturbing educator of men. At
the celebration of Dewey's 70th birthday in 1929,
one of his former students, Ernest Carroll Moore
of the University of California at Los Angeles,
remarked that "Every philosophy has suffered at
the hands of its interpreters. Pythagoras was not
a Pythagorean, Socrates not a Socratic, and
there are those who contend that Christ was not
a Christian. Is this philosophy [Dewey's] to be
the sole exception?" Thirty years later we know
the sad answer to that question. What has hap-
pened to Dewey's popular repute makes urgent

the task of recovering and preserving, before all personal recollections fade and disappear, the authentic stature and flavor of the man.

My own brief experience in Dewey's classroom took place in a graduate course at Teachers College during World War I, just before his departure to lecture in Japan and China. Those were difficult days for a teacher of teachers, with seats emptying daily as students went off to join the armed services. It was not easy, especially in parade-ridden Manhattan, to keep one's mind on the problems of educating the generations to come. For some reason the current traducers of Dewey are fond of portraying him as the incorrigible optimist about human nature, somehow immune to evil and suffering and exempt from the agonies of times of trouble. It is true that, in periods of mass hysteria, Dewey was the least hysterical of men. But such critics forget that he was born only four days after John Brown's raid on Harpers Ferry and that he died one day after Gen. Eisenhower turned over the command of the allied forces in Europe to Gen. Ridgway in 1952. Few Americans have seen more years of crisis and national anxiety than John Dewey.

To discuss Dewey as teacher is to enter a region that abounds in paradoxes. The central one can be stated simply. We know that Dewey has had an immense influence upon education, and not solely through his written words. Literally dozens of his students became pivotal figures in this country's intellectual life. Yet, by all the ordinary criteria, Dewey was a poor teacher. "The mystery," said the late Irwin Edman, who knew him well, "lies in *how* he affected these men." The enigma is not easy to solve. Student after student will tell you that Dewey's teaching

changed the course of his or her thinking fund-
amentally. But each one also will regale you
with tales of his dullness as a lecturer. In fact,
it is almost comical to measure Dewey against
some of his own followers' standards for college
teaching, such as: a magnetic, outgoing personality; evident enthusiasm for his subject; a master of his craft; a clear speaking voice; a fluent
command of English; the ability to hold the
attention, arouse the interest, and enlist the active participation of the student.

In the classroom, Dewey seemed to possess
almost none of these pedagogical essentials.
There were none of the recommended "lecture
techniques" or histrionic devices of the education courses, to say nothing of today's "battery
of visual aids to instruction." His appearance
was farmer-like, weather-beaten, and utterly un-
pretentious. Some of his women students said
that they found it hard, occasionally, to repress
a desire to straighten up his neckties. He remained seated throughout the hour and seldom
seemed to be looking directly at his audience.
Often he would turn in his chair and glance
sideways, as if half-looking out the window and
half-absorbed in his private thoughts. His facial
expression was solemn, though it lighted up at
times with something like a chuckle, and occasionally his hand would ruffle his shock of hair
or tug at his moustache. Questions from the floor
were not exactly discouraged, but they were
not invited.

All these characteristics counted heavily against
John Dewey on the public lecture platform.
There is, of course, the standard legend of his
lecture on "Interest in Education" which put
many of his hearers to sleep. When I came to
Union College in 1925, I found that Dewey's

52

appearance there in 1914 as the deliverer of a course of eight lectures on the Ichabod Spencer Foundation had become a campus legend. In the words of the late Prof. John L. March, Dewey's general topic, "The Psychology of Social Behavior," seemed, "strangely enough, to have little popular appeal." The result was that, although "the lectures were brilliant, and the most able yet given," the audience never filled the college chapel, and at the concluding lecture it had dwindled almost to the vanishing point. Prof. March added the inspired understatement: "Professor Dewey is a quiet talker."

In addition, the style of Dewey's oral as well as written statements was notoriously flat and involved, "lumbering and bumbling" in Edman's words. It provoked Justice Holmes to the famous comment, "So, methought, God would have spoken had He been inarticulate, but keenly desirous to tell you how it was." According to the late Prof. Edward G. Spaulding of Princeton, it once moved William James in conversation to the point of profanity: "Dewey's style," he said, "is damnable; you might even say God-damnable!" In 1942, Max Eastman declared that Dewey had "published 36 books and 815 articles and pamphlets—a pile twelve feet seven inches high—but if he ever wrote one 'quotable' sentence it has got permanently lost in the pile." None of the standard books of quotations (Bartlett, Stevenson, Mencken) contains a single Dewey entry. Yet, in personal conversation, and sometimes in the classroom, the Vermont Yankee's native wit and shrewdness became evident.

How, then, was it possible for Dewey the teacher to be so pre-eminently and abidingly influential? What was the source and secret of his extraordinary power to stir his students to the remaking of their minds? Perhaps the late Ralph Barton Perry came close to blurting out one-half of the answer at the celebration of Dewey's 90th birthday when he said, "He does not feel obliged to live up to his reputation: to be impressive, witty, eloquent, or even interesting; he simply says what he thinks." But what and how did he think? His students came to recognize that an hour listening to Dewey was an exercise in "man thinking." They saw a well-stocked and original mind, remarkably free from any sort of bias or prejudice, engaged in the patient and honest exploration of "whole situations" in experience with the aid of penetrating distinctions and a full-fledged "theory of inquiry."

In the classroom, the student's experience went something like this: The hour opened with a half-revealed abstract pronouncement, an apparent platitude, seldom affording any great air of mystery or suspense. Then would follow a painstaking development of the idea, during which the student was sometimes lulled almost to slumber by the lecturer's snail-like deliberation in getting to the point. But, just as the end of the hour was well in sight, Prof. Dewey would unfold some hitherto-concealed and unexpected practical consequence of his train of thought. Whereupon the student, now completely awake, would curse himself for his inattention and resolve that next time he surely would hang upon every word. One rarely left the classroom without the conviction that something intellectually *and* practically important had been said, no matter how uncertain one was about the precise steps in the argument.

Such classroom experiences might have been

expected to produce fragmentary results. But the thoughtful student learned from Dewey an overwhelming respect for the truly inquiring mind and its rigorous, relentless following of a logical argument wherever it might lead. George Santayana once remarked that "the great difficulty in education is to get experience out of ideas." Dewey as teacher had conquered that difficulty. To his students he was primarily a demonstrator of method, of the power of abstract theory when harnessed to the mastery of complex, concrete situations. Far from being hasty, or sketchy, or undisciplined in his thinking, Dewey's forte was the setting of an example of the rarest sort of disciplined mind—the kind which could cope with a changing world.

Fortunately, Dewey himself set forth the secret behind his power as a teacher:

I have usually, if not always, held an idea first in its abstract form, often as a matter chiefly of logical or dialectic consistency or of the power of words to suggest ideas. Some personal experience, through contact with individuals, groups, or (as in foreign countries) peoples, was necessary to give the idea concrete significance. There are no ideas which are original in substance, but a common substance is given a new expression when it operates through the medium of individual temperament and the peculiar, unique incidents of an individual life. . . . My ideas tend, because of my temperament, to take a schematic form in which logical consistency is a dominant consideration, but I have been fortunate in a variety of contacts that has put substance into these forms. The fruits of responsiveness in these matters have confirmed ideas first aroused on more technical grounds of philosophical study. My belief in the office of intelligence as a continuously reconstructive agency is at least a faithful report of my own life and experience.[1]

The respect of Dewey's students for his words flowed from two convictions about their nature. The first was that he had a firm grasp upon the abstractions involved and their logical implications; and the second was that he was thinking to some purpose and some ultimate test in practice. Those who learned the most from Dewey as teacher have not been those who have begun with his particular conclusions and turned them into esoteric jargon or popular slogans. They are, rather, those who have attempted to follow his example in their own individual fashions. That has involved the avoidance of what Whitehead called "inert ideas" in favor of the dynamic variety and the continuous facing of unsolved problems in all their bewildering complexity. It also has called for the renunciation of any expectation of easy or permanent solutions. A humanity that is fully alive never will run out of the need of fresh, hard, comprehensive thinking. As Dewey himself once said, "The most Utopian thing about Utopia is that in it there are no schools." Hence, our distance from Utopia always can be used as the measure of our need for schooling.

As the figure of John Dewey the teacher commences its second 100 years of impact upon a sluggish humanity, forever weary of the hard labor of thinking, there are those who will argue with some cogency that many of his thoughts in the heyday of liberalism, before it degenerated into its present uneasy complacency, are much too sanguine for us to entertain. That verdict would not have disturbed Dewey, who wanted

---

[1] In P. A. Schilpp, editor, "The Philosophy of John Dewey," second edition (New York, 1951), pp. 44-45.

us above all to think for ourselves, for our time, and for the future. There could be no greater folly than to dismiss him as a quaint exemplar of outmoded Yankee virtues or a typical 19th-century museum piece. For, although he was not unmindful of his predecessors, Dewey's whole orientation was toward the future. As between him and his detractors, the future will decide, and no former student of his will have any doubts about the outcome. As Irwin Edman has said, "The race is still between intelligence and catastrophe. His was a voice for reasonable-ness and for imagination. He will be listened to again and long."

Science, Ethics, and Education in Dewey's Philosophy[1]

By ISAAC B. BERKSON

My INTRODUCTION to Dewey came in my undergraduate days through "Ethics," which he wrote with James A. Tufts. From this early experience I carried away four related ideas which have remained fundamental in my outlook: that ethics was central in philosophy—a conception which acted as confirmation of the religious heritage I brought from my home; that ethics dealt not only with individual conduct but also indivisibly with social life; that the social-ethical thesis required, unavoidably, a serious consideration of economic issues and labor problems; and that morality demanded thought—deliberate consideration of probable consequences—and not simply good will and firm intention. The last idea I fully accepted, but I did not think it meant—nor do I think that Dewey intended that it should mean—lack of regard for clear moral principles or for definitely formulated social goals.

Subsequent study of Dewey's writings confirmed in my mind, as Dewey explained in a later summary, that "the social aspect of education was always put first."[2] "Democracy and Education" (1916), which for a considerable period

[1] Based on an address at the 15th Annual Meeting, Philosophy of Education Society, March 25, 1959, and published in the *Proceedings*.

[2] In K. C. Mayhew and A. C. Edwards, "The Dewey School" (New York: Appleton-Century, 1936), p. 467.

represented the fullest exposition of Dewey's general philosophy as well as of his educational thought, begins with a discussion of the relation of education to community survival and renewal. The definition of education as "continuous growth with no end beyond itself," an idea I now consider a stumbling block to the needed reformulation of educational theory, received its original and extreme expression in this book. But, in the light of my general orientation, I read this at the time as related to personal development within the framework of a community life and not as an all-sufficient definition of educational purpose as it sometimes has been interpreted. In "Democracy and Education" also, Dewey gives a lead to the development of "the reconstructionist" educational philosophy. In a memorable statement, he says that "the reconstruction of philosophy, of education, and of social ideals and methods . . . go [sic] hand in hand."[3]

With the ethical-and-social, the personality-and-community aspects of the Deweyan philosophy I fully agree. Moreover, I continue to value the emphasis on experience and on empirical method in the pragmatist tradition common to Dewey, James, and Peirce. But I have come to have serious doubts about the tenability of experimentalism as Dewey finally expounded it, i.e., as an all-embracing unitary method equally valid for all areas of knowing—moral as well as scientific, esthetic as well as intellectual. With this epistemological view are linked the guiding ideas of educational experimentalism, e.g., the hypothesis of change and activity as pervasive features, the definition of education in terms

---

[3] J. Dewey, "Democracy and Education" (New York: Macmillan, 1916), p. 386.

of process and growth, the opposition to "*a priori* judgments" and "fixed ends" and the confident reliance in moral issues, on the primary experience of the individual. The opposition to the experimentalist conception has been attributed by the followers of Dewey at times to loose applications by the more extreme advocates of Progressive education. There has been, no doubt, a great deal of misunderstanding, of one-sided adaptation, and even of distortion in the utilization of the Deweyan ideas. But because of so much misinterpretation, there is room for the suspicion that there may be something the matter with the experimentalist doctrine itself. Two aspects of the experimentalist epistemology as presented by Dewey seem especially open to criticism:[4] a partial—and hence, in total effect, incorrect—analysis of the nature of scientific method in which too exclusive an emphasis is laid on the operational procedures in scientific inquiry with the consequence that the conceptual elements receive inadequate attention; and an insistence that the experimentalist "method of intelligence," which is equated with "the scientific method," is valid for all types of knowing and that it is to be relied upon for the resolution of problems in the sphere of morals as well as in the field of the natural sciences.

Dewey's purpose, as stated in "The Quest for Certainty," is to bring about "the realization that intelligent action is the sole ultimate resource of mankind in every field whatsover" (p. 252). By "intelligent action" he means the experimental approach which has brought about the great

---

[4] For Dewey's exposition and defense of his view, see P. A. Schilpp, editor, "The Philosophy of John Dewey" (Evanston: Northwestern University, 1939), especially pp 520-529, 578-591.

advances in modern times in the natural sciences. Moreover, his insistence on the identification of all intelligent action with mode of scientific inquiry is coupled with his sustained endeavor to abolish the traditional dualism in philosophic thought—the separation of intellectual apprehension from common-sense knowledge, or, as he expresses it in the frame of his doctrine of experience, "the isolation of cognitive experience" from other modes of experience—esthetic, moral, practical—particularly from the ordinary experience of men in the daily life. A common element in scientific inquiry and ordinary learning experiences is the presence of operational procedures; in both areas thought is always closely related in one way or another to action.

In this analysis there appears to be the following underestimation of the part played by abstract thought in the development of the sciences: failure to give due weight to previously accumulated organized knowledge and formulated principles; and inadequate consideration of speculative, imaginative constructions but little related to direct experience, or even which seem to contradict the usual experience. Dewey, of course, is aware of such factors—achievements of past experiences and vision of future possibilities—and occasionally he mentions them. But his failure to give adequate consideration to the conceptual aspects of the mind amounts, in practice, to a neglect of them. His dominant interest in change, process, and growth leads, unintentionally perhaps, to depreciate the value of enduring ideas and structural beliefs which direct, as well as condition, all thinking. A particular example of this is the paucity of attention to deductive forms of reasoning, especially the part that pure mathematics has played in the development of the physical sciences.

Our knowledge of nature, no doubt, rests on observation, is stimulated by the need of solving practical problems, and is not clinched except through empirical or experimental verification. But science, after all, is far removed from common-sense experience. The discoveries of modern physics would have been impossible without the mediation of the Pythagorean insight that "all things are number," that the universe of nature can be understood only with the aid of quantitative conceptions. All important advances in scientific theory in modern times, through Galileo, Newton and Einstein, have been accompanied or preceded by the acceptance of a mathematical approach or by advances in mathematical science. And mathematical advance, though certainly not unrelated to ordinary experience and practical problems, is inconceivable without the assumption that the human being possesses something in the nature of a sixth sense—the faculty of direct apprehension of forms and relations.

In line with his naturalistic pre-suppositions, Dewey finds the roots of culture in the biological equipment of man. He tends to represent ideas as arising in the course of man's pursuit of life activities; gross experience is made to appear as prior and prerequisite to the refined experience of mental activity. But man, as Ernest Cassirer has taught, is an *animal symbolicum*. It is true that man is conditioned by his animality; his distinctiveness, nevertheless, lies in the fact that he is an imaginative being who, from the very beginning of his existence as a human being, has looked upon his universe with the eye of the mind.

The nature of man cannot be understood from

the study of his biological impulsions primarily. The essence of man can only be indirectly inferred by tracing back from his cultural achievements in science and art, in philosophy and religion, and in political and social institutions. In all of these, constructive imagination—conceptualized principles, envisioned design, abstract theories—has played a creative part. In the beginning of civilization was the symbol, the meaningful word, the directing idea. No absolute separation between thought and experience is here implied. Thought and experience depend on each other and interact with each other. But thought is not to be regarded merely as "experience reflected upon"; it also is to be conceived as "chastened imagination," as imagination disciplined by logic as well as by experience. Thinking is not only "intelligent action"; it involves the formulation of ideas, and keeping them in mind as ideas.

Revision of the experimentalist conception of the nature of knowledge and intelligence along the lines suggested above should lead to a reconsideration of the progressivist innovations in curriculum organization and intellectual discipline. Without disregarding the valuable contributions made in the "unit-of-work" and "project" techniques as auxiliary modes of teaching, the criticisms made above imply a retention of the more traditional forms of instruction, *e.g.*, the division of the course of study into subjects or broad areas, emphasis on knowledge content and on general principles, and regard for precision, clarity, and consistency. But the implications of the analysis go beyond pedagogical emendations; they reach to the heart of Dewey's ethical theory—to his persevering effort to deny what he termed "the Kantian dualism of scientific and moral knowing." To the very end, in his reply to critics, he continued to defend the doctrine of "the supremacy of method," explaining that it was identical with his contention that the method of intelligence, patterned on scientific method, was as indispensable in the formulation of moral ends as it was in the pursuit of knowledge of physical nature.

No absolute wall of separation can be maintained properly between science and morals. Scientific findings may influence our conceptions of values, and moral considerations may limit our experiments on human beings. Nevertheless, the traditional belief that there is a significant distinction between the two spheres seems well grounded. In science, verification is possible, but we cannot verify moral judgments. If we make an assertion about a fact of nature, we can go to nature to find whether our assertion is true. If we know how to formulate the question and can arrange a proper experiment, we possibly can educe the needed verification. With man's aid, nature is competent to answer questions about herself.

But how can we validate our moral judgments? Certainly not by turning to nature which permits the sun to shine on the sinner and the righteous alike. To judge by the consequences? Is this not a mere begging of the question? Does not the judgment by consequences involve a prior criterion of value by which the judgment is made? That cyanide gas will kill is a fact that easily can be verified; but how can we decide whether the extermination of millions of men in the gas chambers of concentration camps is good or evil unless we have a prior commitment to the idea that life and liberty are inalienable rights? We must face the fact that moral judgments are human opinions; they cannot be true or false, only good or bad, better or worse. To decide whether they are good or bad, better or worse, we again must refer to human opinion.

I see only one way out of the dilemma if we are to avoid the morass of subjectivism: start with the values and beliefs of the communities to which we belong.

Scientific judgments, to be sure, also depend on the prior acceptance of principles historically developed and supported by a consensus of investigators. But the scientific consensus has the possibility of being verified by objective reference to natural phenomena. A scientific consensus is not a voluntary agreement arrived at by discussion and compromise; it is, in Buchler's words, a "compelled agreement," compelled by the evidence of the investigation. Moral principles have only the experience of a historical community—of a church, of a school of philosophy, of a nation, or of a civilization—to support them. Insofar as a system of ethics represents a consensus, it is in essence a voluntary, a conventional, agreement. The difference between scientific validation and moral justification might be expressed as the difference between a test and testimony. In science we may have verification by experimental test; in morals we can, at most, have testimony—the testimony of prophets and saints, of philosophers and statesmen, the testimony offered by long experience voiced in literature, the testimony of the values and ideals to which, as members of the human community, we respond.

The individual as individual cannot be a moral person. Moral judgments are possible only insofar as we consider ourselves members of communities. And as Dewey well says in the opening chapters of "Democracy and Education." "What we must have in common in order to form a community are aims, beliefs, aspirations, knowledge—a common understanding. . . ." Moral judgments require the prior commitment to common assumptions and common ideals. In a democratic society, the individual has a measure of free choice—to reject some elements in the tradition, to modify what he accepts; his greatest right is to follow the ideal of his community as a means of advancing the welfare of his community. He also has the right to change his community affiliation; but then to be a moral person he must affiliate with another community and accept another body of principles.

Such a community conception of the nature of the moral personality is in consonance with—indeed, inherent in—Dewey's social approach to culture and education. But the ethical force of Dewey's teaching has been counteracted by the experimentalist philosophy with its strong impingement of 19th-century motifs: the evolutionary biological theme, the impulse toward liberation from the burden of the past, the centrality of the individual. Despite Dewey's continual asseveration that the individual is a social being, the individual tends to stand out as an entity in himself. Emphasis is laid on individual thinking; the fact that thinking is not possible, on any significant level, without the mediation of concepts, unchanging for the while, receives scant attention. All the essentials of community life—that "social" necessarily implies institutional organization; that "socialization" means *belonging* to definite communities, as well as association with other individuals; that "belonging" involves loyalty and obligation

—all somehow get lost in the course of the discussion.

Revision of the Deweyan philosophy requires both thoroughgoing consideration to the institutional aspects of the term "social" and explicit recognition of the central part that conscious ideas play in intelligent action and moral conduct. These lines of revision imply abandoning the attempt to derive human purposes from a study of man's natural tendencies. A study of the nature and needs of the child has pedagogical importance and, in some measure, is relevant also for defining the aims of education, since, in a sense, the child is father to the man. But, essentially, the study of the child is truly significant only insofar as his nature and needs are seen in the framework of, and in relation to, the character of the society of which he is to become a member.

The clue to man's true nature is to be found in man's highest cultural attainments. If education is to be conceived of as growth, it is to be thought of not as the development of his biological tendencies with no end in view, but as growth *toward* the cultural achievements, toward the ideals of the community. This means that the study of education begins with the study of the existing culture, its heritage of traditions, its possibilities, and its problems; it begins with positive ends and with ideals toward which to strive. The doctrine of "education as growth with no end beyond itself" cannot stand. The concept "growth" has value in its admonition against mechanistic learning processes; it has constructive implications also for personal development within the framework of community purposes. But, when it is used as an all-embracing directive and as a means of denying the need of definite aims for the educational endeavor, it becomes a negative, even a disintegrating, principle.

Education must be rooted in the cultural heritage of a community; its aims are to be found in the intellectual and artistic achievements, in the traditions and ideals, in the ethical aspirations and political organization developed in the course of time. This is true whether we think of education as a means of individual development or of social preservation. The self, which always retains a sense of uniqueness, never can be realized fully within the institutional organization. But if the self is to develop at all, it can do so only through participation in a community life and through identification with a pattern of ideas.

Notoriously, the cultural heritage contains a mixture of evil and good; it perpetuates outworn beliefs along with scientific knowledge; it supports narrow prejudices as well as universal conceptions. A prime function of the school as the deliberate educational agency is to select from the cultural composite these elements that have significance, to transmit to the new generation the highest achievements in the fields of knowledge, to widen the sense of community and to deepen the sense of responsibility and to cultivate the ideal which society professes. This never can be merely a transmission from the past. The school always will have a double function. One we may call "acculturation," bringing the individual up to the level approved by the existing society. The other we term "idealization," the effort to lift society toward its own ideal, which it avows but has not yet adequately embodied in its institutions. The pursuit of the ideal must make us face the future, so that to the conservationist purpose of the school we must add its reconstructionist function. This is particularly true today as we undeniably confront the emergence of a new world order.

Education demands a choice of ends and values. The primary responsibility for defining the principles and purposes of education must rest on the professors of educational philosophy. Philosophy of education does not fulfill its function merely by analysis and criticism. Philosophy begins with analysis and criticism of existing formulations of beliefs, but it also must reformulate beliefs which are logically well ordered, consonant with new knowledge, and effective in advancing the growing ideal of the community which the philosopher represents. Whatever else the philosopher does—and there is much auxiliary work in the clarification and the formulation of beliefs—it is valuable in the measure that it aids in laying a basis of assumptions and formulating educational aims. The needed principles and ideals are not only scientific and intellectual, but also moral and social; and social means political and, to some extent, economic.

Such a conception of the purpose of a philosophy of education I find embedded in the writings of John Dewey. In the earlier days of his career, he believed that the necessary social reconstruction would come indirectly, through the influence of communal environment of the school on the growing individual. In the crisis decade of the 1930's, he joined with John L. Childs in the thesis, "Education must itself assume an increasing responsibility for participation in projecting ideas of social change and taking part in their execution in order to be educative." It is in this essay, too, that criteria for choice in a democratic educational philosophy are set down: "Does the choice depend on a survey and interpretation which discloses existing social conditions and trends? . . . Does it sense and formulate the deeper and more intangible aspirations, purposes and values, for an educational philosophy, in our own American scene and life?"[5]

To the phrase "American scene and life," I would add—in complete harmony with the spirit of the Deweyan declaration—the phrase "Western civilization." To fulfill the purposes of education in our era of transition, we dare not, for a moment, see America as isolated from its worldwide connection and from its historical evolution. We must envisage America, today, as an integral part of a developing world-order; and we must view it in the perspective of the complex of ideas which we rightly call "the Western tradition"—a tradition which incorporates the Judeo-Christian ethical and spiritual heritage; the Hellenic love of reason, of music, and of art; and the Roman sense of law in its double aspect of positive and natural law. To these principles we must add the modern scientific approach—in the things that belong to science. Capping all is the principle of democracy which we should see not only as a political and social methodology, but as an ethical system based on a trinity of human absolutes—the unique individual person, the equality of all races, and the unity of mankind.

As in all other philosophies, there are transient as well as enduring elements in the Deweyan conception. Whether we agree with the experimentalist analysis of scientific method and its relation to morals is of relatively secondary im-

---

[5] In W. H. Kilpatrick, editor, "The Educational Frontier" (New York: Appleton-Century, 1933), p. 319.

portance. The enduring element can be appreciated only as we view Dewey's philosophy as a whole in its three-fold aspect—the ethical-social striving which pervades it, the emphasis on the use of mind as well as will in furthering the good life, and the recognition of the importance of education in the formation of personality and in the advance of the good society. In this conjunction of aims Dewey exemplifies Western philosophy in its authentic and fully elaborated form—the pattern of philosophy which found its first clear expression in Plato's "Republic." Only as we view Dewey's lifelong endeavor, in the light of man's unending struggle to establish a political order based on justice as a means of releasing man's potentialities for a life of mind and spirit, can we recognize the true import of his rich and many-sided contribution.

Dewey's Culture Theory and Pedagogy[1]

By ROBERT E. MASON

JOHN DEWEY'S thought, like that of any man who faces squarely the intellectual and cultural tensions of his age, must be understood in the light of those tensions. Dewey was a liberal. As such, he was opposed to arbitrary imposition of externally determined standards upon the lives of men. It is understandable, therefore, that when he directed attention to pedagogical problems, techniques for freeing the young from imposition held special appeal. The growing individual was to be given a part to play in determining the controls which were to guide his own nurture. The nature of the child was to be considered and given high respect in formulation of pedagogical policy and practice. Thus, we find that Dewey's earlier writings emphasize the role which psychology has to play in guiding educational practice. He wrote, in 1897,

I believe that this educational process has two sides—one psychological and one sociological. . . . Of these two sides, the psychological is the basis. The child's own instincts and powers furnish the material and give the starting-point for all education.[2]

Nearly two decades later, in "Democracy and Education," Dewey makes abundantly clear that what had been referred to as "the child's own instincts and powers" are not naturally given but

---

[1] Based on a paper presented to the Philosophy of Education Section, National Society of College Teachers of Education, Chicago, Feb. 12, 1959.

[2] J. Dewey, "The Pedagogical Creed of Professor John Dewey," in O. H. Lang, editor, "Educational Creeds of the Nineteenth Century" (New York: Kellogg, 1898), p. 6.

are themselves culturally produced, that ". . . social environment forms the mental and emotional disposition of behavior in individuals. . . ."[3] Nevertheless, in this and in subsequent writings there are apparent differences in the manner in which Dewey uses the term *experience* to refer to the substance of mental and emotional disposition. Sometimes *experience* is interpreted as something a person *has*. Consequently, experience is viewed from the stance of the developing individual. Thus,

Experience is primarily a process of undergoing: a process of standing something; of suffering and passion, of affection, in the literal sense of these words. The organism has to endure, to undergo, the consequences of its own actions.[4]

But in other instances, experience is objectified as that which sustains all processes of undergoing and enduring. Thus,

When we say that experience is one point of approach to an account of the world in which we live, we mean then by experience something at least as wide and deep and full as all history on this earth. . . .[5]

The conception of education as reconstruction of experience includes both dimensions. In the notion that there is always some experience present (hence, the use of the term *re*construction), we have the recognition of experience as something a person has. In the notion that this is reconstructed through social participation, we have the recognition of something external to the individual making impact upon and taking effect in the growth and development of the person.

[3] J. Dewey, "Democracy and Education" (New York: Macmillan, 1916), p. 19.
[4] J. Dewey, in "Creative Intelligence" (New York: Holt, 1917), p. 10.
[5] J. Dewey, "Experience and Nature" (Chicago: Open Court, 1925), p. 8.

But what was somehow never made clear—at least to the point where it was understood and applied in the preparation of teachers—was that the very content both of educative experience and of the personality of the candidate for such experiencing are cultural products to be located in the culture. Or, again, it was not made clear —to the extent that those preparing teachers took it seriously—that the learner learns the culture with whatever the culture has provided him. For instance, recall Kilpatrick's fundamental principal of pedagogy that we learn what we live and live what we learn. It would seem to follow that the way to understand learners so as to direct their learning effectively is to understand the culture which has built their lives. Yet, Kilpatrick finds it necessary to say, in 1942,

> Children must learn the essentials of the group culture or they cannot live the group life. The culture thus sets the first great task of education. But we must say in immediate connection that if the culture sets the aim of education, it is psychology that fixes the method.[6]

It is difficult to reconcile this assertion with a theory that personality is wrought out of a specific cultural milieu. If the culture produces the person, it would seem that educational method as much as educational aims must be seen as grounded in the character of a culture. This way, it may be questioned whether psychology can any more fix the method of education than it can the aims.

The professional significance of the apparent dichotomy is to be discovered in a characteristic split between those who come at educational

---

[6] W. H. Kilpatrick, "Philosophy of Education from the Experimentalist Outlook," in N. B. Henry, editor, "Philosophies of Education," Forty-first Yearbook, National Society for the Study of Education, Part I (Chicago: University of Chicago Press, 1942), p. 62.

policy from a psychological and from a cultural point of view. As if the two sides identified by Dewey in 1897 had never found satisfactory reconciliation, a persisting tendency is for a kind of running feud in Schools of Education between "the psychologists" and the "social foundations people" in their efforts to build with intellectual integrity a design for the professional preparation of teachers. The psychologically oriented educationists have been preoccupied with the effort to discover laws and principles of learning and teaching which are most generally applicable. While they have reiterated that children are different and that individual differences must be recognized in teaching, they fail to provide realistic directives to go along with the maxims. Instead, teachers in training are given the impression that developmental psychology is the key that unlocks all doors. Thus, in contemporary literature, the fascinating social research of the Chicago group—Warner, Havighurst, Davis, and company—when finally applied to pedagogy becomes Havighurst's *developmental tasks*, the basic categories of which are biological, psychological, individualistic.

Institutions for the preparation of teachers do not ordinarily differentiate whether a candidate is preparing to work in a village in the southern Ohio hills, in a big city's middle-class suburb, or in a central area school close to the industrial heart of the city. The preparation of teachers differentiates according to age level and, to some extent, the subject which the teacher expects to teach. But it is assumed, apparently, that other sorts of limitations and controls do not matter. If we see cultural differences constituting the limitations, controls, and the very substantial media of creative thought, the failure to make systematic study of them a central part of teacher education is a failure to give attention to the media of creative work. Certainly an artist or craftsman, trained in the abstract without constant attention to the media in which the work is to be done, is, indeed, one without preparation. Such a training program is absurd—unthinkable.

What is development? What is maturation? With a different cultural orientation, development of conceptual thought itself might be suspect. The ancient Spartans had one of the most efficient school systems in history but paid little or no attention to development of verbal-social skills. The point is that the criteria in terms of which development is judged are criteria only because the culture, or a segment of the culture, has placed a value upon them.

If we take this cultural approach to education seriously, we view children and young people living and learning with their entire bodies, and with the culture in which they are growing up. That is, we think of a person as a complex of preferences and avoidances built up out of where he has lived, the civilization in which he has been nurtured, and the religion to which he is bound. All of that is him. This way, literally, a child is his body, his house, his social class, his religion. Thus, if the mission of teachers is to facilitate learning, the substance of educational diagnosis is social diagnosis. Understanding food habits, religious, social, and economic forces, and street-corner society in the neighborhood may be at least as important as understanding an M.A. score on a psychological test or an achievement test profile.

When it is seen that the growing and developing of children is a cultural phenomenon, basing a school program on the so-called developmental tasks of children may be deemed inadequate. For it will be questioned whether research on child development in New Haven can be transferred directly to an elementary school or a high school in a Cleveland, Columbus, or Chicago neighborhood. We support Allison Davis in his statement:

Our knowledge of social class training and of the biological and psychological differentials in child development as between class environments is now sufficient to enable us to say that no studies can henceforth generalize about *"the* child." We shall always have to ask, "A child of what class, in what environment?"[7]

The places, the ethnic traditions, the clashing values, the social and economic strivings which constitute the lives of pupils on the streets, on the playgrounds, and in the homes which make up school neighborhoods are educational media. We are reminded that our town, our neighborhood, our city form an organization of physical things in space. We are reminded that it is a way of life—that is, a way of begetting and food-gathering and wedding and dying. Finally, we are reminded that it is a complexity of ideals and values in the form of ethnic, religious, and political traditions. Thus, we are reminded that to teach children in our town as if our town were like any other is unrealistic and artificial. For we know that effective teaching is that which facilitates the growth and extension of creative critical intelligence, seen as reconstruction of experience. Learning, then, is viewed as creative reconstruction of experience, the cultural milieu in which students are living as the raw material,

[7] W. A. Davis, "American Status Systems and the Socialization of the Child," Chapter 33, in C. Kluckhohn and H. A. Murray, editors, "Personality in Nature, Society, and Culture" (New York: Knopf, 1949), p. 466.

the medium, upon which intelligence is exercised.

In the cultural approach to educational work, there exists one of the more promising frontiers for American education. Moreover, in such an approach many of the fundamental issues of the great mid-century educational controversy might be clarified. No claim is made that a shift from the psychological to the social foundations of education in preparing American teachers is one which would resolve all issues and finally bring about an era of peace and understanding in American education. But the claim may be made that in the cultural approach to education, taken seriously, a fresh and perhaps somewhat more productive approach is provided.

This way—that is, building squarely on the social, philosophical, and historical foundations —the sources of educational values are two-fold. In the first place, certain elemental human satisfactions broadly shared in society are taken as ends. Many years ago, Morris Raphael Cohen put it this way:

> What makes human life dignified and worthwhile are not the instrumentalities but certain things which are ends in themselves, the delights of companionship, the joy of creative activity, the vision of beauty, and not least the unique privilege of being for a brief space a spectator of the great drama of existence in which solar systems are born and destroyed—a drama in which our part as actors is of infinitesimal significance.[8]

But values such as these, inescapably fundamental as they are, are not held unconditionally, for there are the claims of the intellectual, social, and institutional tools and methods by which such values are achieved. Thus, a second source of educational values is in the preservation and extension of human intelligence. Its

[8] M. R. Cohen, *New Republic*, 8: 119, Sept. 2, 1916.

claim is, in a sense, a mediated or indirect one, inasmuch as its selection is made in the light of alternatives. The relationship and the claim are like those which exist between a tool and an artifact to the building of which the tool contributes. For example, one decides to go to Los Angeles. This becomes the goal or value. He decides to drive to Los Angeles and invests the money he has laid aside for the purpose to purchase an automobile. The automobile becomes the tool for realizing the value (*i.e.*, arrival in Los Angeles). Once this is done, however, the preservation of the tool becomes an instrumental value but one with claims fully as demanding as the prior one chosen as an end. Thus, one delays arrival in Los Angeles to have the car serviced. He spends money on the car which he would have preferred to spend in Los Angeles. The *means* comes to have its own claims, because it is seen as the tool for achieving the end.

In the same fashion, the methods of free inquiry, its arduous disciplines, and the preservation of social conditions which it demands for its functioning have value as means and must be preserved and extended in the name of the values which make up the good life for men. Thus, since methods of critical intelligence are seen as the way by which men may achieve their ends, they are preserved and treasured. In times of crisis, reasonable men, then, because of their conviction that intelligence is a tool of great value, suffer starvation, exposure, illness, loneliness, and drudgery to preserve it. They do this in the conviction that if the free mind yields to power, the means for achieving the good life have been destroyed.

Inasmuch as the school is devoted to the nurture of the young in those skills, insights, and understandings which promise human satisfactions, disciplined intelligence becomes the central concern. The concern, then, is to extend the methods, outlook, skills, and loyalties of intelligent living and, in the process, to maximize human satisfactions. Human values, such as those of food, clothing, shelter, family life, health, companionship, and adventure, are to be achieved and realized through the practical exercise of disciplined intelligence. Two questions, then, must always be asked when it is proposed to include something in a school program: How will this contribute to human satisfaction and what will this do for people? How will this contribute to the intellectual development of free men?

These questions we ask when it is proposed to teach Chaucer, Latin declensions, the United Nations Charter, swimming, solid geometry, social dancing, agriculture, vocal music, religion. But inasmuch as there are a vast number of possible things to teach not altogether worthless, the questions come to be rephrased as directing choice among alternatives, thus: Will teaching this now contribute more to human satisfaction —to the good life for these people—than teaching something else now? Will teaching this now contribute more effectively to intellectual development of these people than teaching something else now?

Obviously, these questions cannot be answered critically by one person with ready ease. For the answer to the first question depends upon criteria of satisfaction alive in the culture under consideration and the special hazards to decent living existing in the culture. In some parts of the world now, the study of hookworm and dysentery might be given a very high priority, but in most parts of the U.S. today these subjects would have a low priority in terms of the criteria laid down. This means, apparently, that only on the ground of intensive study of the cultural situation can intelligent proposals for the school curriculum be made. Only after intensive social diagnosis can we determine which studies most need to be emphasized in schools.

To answer the second question as rephrased requires a somewhat different kind of scholarship. The activity of disciplined intelligence is a kind of artistic activity, in the sense that it must always be exercised upon something. That is, we only learn to think as we think about something. Or, again, there must be a medium upon which thought is exercised. Thus, one consideration is whether the proposed subject of inquiry is at hand. Is this a subject which is present in the lives of the people? Is it here so that it can be worked upon? Since there must be a present medium in order for an art to be practiced, the more remote a subject from the daily lives of people, the more difficult it is to achieve critical thinking about it. This difficulty has been dramatized in world political misunderstandings. Another example may well be the misunderstandings and difficulties surrounding desegregation of schools in the American South. The answer to the second question also requires an intimate knowledge of the intellectual, social, and emotional maturity of those who are expected to study the subject. Appreciation of literature can scarcely be taught to illiterates. Relativity physics can scarcely be handled critically by people who do not know mathematics.

If decisions about the work of the schools should be made in some such fashion as that outlined above, then the task of deciding what schools ought to be doing is a scholarly task of enormous magnitude. The resources of scholarship in sociology, economics, social psychology, and anthropology are needed to achieve competently grounded understanding of community cultures. This knowledge must be fused with grounded insights into the order and integration of knowledge to arrive at determinations of learnings deserving highest priority in specific schools with various groups of young people. If this task is to be managed effectively, it is imperative that the entire community of scholars devote attention to the work of the schools. Teachers, school administrators, and professors of education cannot do the job alone.

If the public school controversy means that academic scholars are becoming ready to participate responsibly in educational research and policy-making, that is all to the good. But until scholars take the time to devote themselves to studies of the order and integration of knowledge in the context of specific cultural situations, they are guilty of irresponsible talk as they make proposals for the work of schools. Intensive study of societies and familiarity with the fields of human knowledge are demanded. The contributions of scholars from all fields are needed, but their contributions will be vitiated unless they are willing to engage themselves in sober and systematic study of the living culture of the men who are to be educated, giving full respect to the visions of the good life held by the masses of men.

John Dewey and Progressive Education Today

By M. I. BERGER

It is IRONICAL that John Dewey remains today at the center of a conflict in American education. The man who dedicated himself to the task of reconciling apparently antithetical positions in education provoked a new era of conflict. There are several reasons why Dewey became and has remained a controversial figure in education. First, the obscurity of some of his writing led many to misunderstand him. Second, there were many who, sincerely believing they were following the ideas of Dewey, brought forth new conceptions that contradicted or went far away from Dewey's own belief. (In part, Dewey is to blame for this development, since he left many questions unanswered. Indeed, his educational writings left the explicit consequences of his ideas for others to devise.) Nevertheless, these ideas, although they often did not agree with the philosopher's notions, were identified with his conception of education. Finally, there are many who have attacked Dewey but never have bothered to read and examine his meanings.

What was Dewey's educational position? The most common fallacy is that Dewey is the father of Progressive education and, consequently, is responsible for all that emerged from this movement. Actually, Progressive education was, in great measure, independent of Dewey's ideas. Many would be startled to know that Dewey devoted a large part of his efforts to criticizing the basic assumptions of Progressive educators. One of the most important contributions of the American philosopher was that he tried to reconcile the split between Progressivists and Traditionalists by showing that both philosophies were vital and proper in the scheme of education. There are two works of the man that clearly show him trying to reconcile these differences: "The Child and the Curriculum" (1902) and "Experience and Education" (1938).

Which is more important in education, the child or the curriculum? Progressivists would say the child with all his needs and interests should be respected above all else; personality and character, freedom and initiative, spontaneity, and change—these are the keynotes of the Progressive theme. Traditionalists, on the other hand, emphasize the curriculum, the heritage of the past, the funded experiences of mankind; knowledge and information, guidance and discipline, the old and the past—these values stream from the traditionalists. Dewey, in "The Child and the Curriculum," says both schools of thought, in their proper places, are correct:

Abandon the notion of subject matter as something fixed and ready-made in itself, outside the child's experience; cease thinking of the child's experience as also something hard and fast; see it as something fluent, embryonic, vital; and we realize that the child and the curriculum are simply two limits which define a single process. Just as two points define a straight line, so the present standpoint of the child and the facts and truths of studies define instruction. It is continuous reconstrucion moving from the child's present experience out into that represented by the organized bodies of truth we call studies (p. 11).

For Dewey, then, both the child and the curriculum are important in the educative process. The problem is not that of choosing one or the other but devising a way to bring the child with all his experiences to understand and assimilate the wealth of our culture. He continues,

. . . The radical fallacy . . . is that we have no choice save either to leave the child to his own unguided spontaneity or to inspire direction upon him from without. Action is response; it is adaptation, adjustment. There is no such thing as sheer self activity possible—because all activity takes place in a medium, in a situation, and with reference to its conditions. But, again, no such thing as imposition of truth from without, as insertion of truth from within, is possible. All depends upon the activity which the mind itself undergoes in responding to what is presented from without. Now the value of the formulated wealth of knowledge that makes up the course of study is that it may enable the educator *to determine the environment of the child,* and thus by indirection to direct. Its primary value, its primary indication, is for the teacher, not for the child. It says to the teacher: Such and such are the capacities, the fulfilments, in truth and beauty and behavior, open to these children. Now see to it that day by day the conditions are such that *their own activities* move inevitably in this direction, toward such culmination of themselves. Let the child's nature fulfil its own destiny, revealed to you in whatever of science and art and industry the world now holds as its own (pp. 30-31).

Dewey was trying to move away from the formulation of educational problems in terms of an Either-Or philosophy. As stated, traditional and Progressive education, in their proper context, are appropriate. Just as surely, both philosophies, when falsely stressed, are wrong. Traditional education, when it emphasized the curriculum without regard for the learner, made a mistake. Progressive education, when it devoted all its energies to the child and ignored all external authority, when it ignored the importance of subject matter, was equally wrong. As Dewey states in "Experience and Education,"

. . . When external authority is rejected, the problem becomes that of finding the factors of control that are inherent within experience. When external authority is rejected, it does not follow that all authority should be rejected, but rather that there is need to search for a more effective source of authority. Because the older education imposed the knowledge, methods, and rules of conduct of the mature person upon the young, it does not follow, except on the basis of the extreme Either-Or philosophy, that the knowledge and skill of the mature person have no directive value for the experience of the immature. On the contrary, basing education upon personal experience may mean more multiplied and more intimate contacts between the mature and the immature than ever existed in the traditional school, and consequently more, rather than less, guidance by others . . . (p. 8).

Above all else, Dewey continues, it is wrong to attach allegiance to any philosophy because of its name. Neither Progressive nor traditional education is unquestionably good. The only worthy cause is that of improving education.

I have used frequently . . . the words "progressive" and "new" education. I do not wish to close, however, without recording my firm belief that the fundamental issue is not of new versus old education nor of progressive against traditional education but a question of what anything whatever must be to be worthy of the name *education*. I am not, I hope and believe, in favor of any ends or any methods simply because the name progressive may be applied to them. The basic question concerns the nature of education with no qualifying adjectives prefixed. What we want and need is education pure and simple, and shall make surer and faster progress when we devote ourselves to finding out just what education is and what conditions have to be satisfied in order that education may be a reality and not a name or a slogan . . . (pp. 115-116). /

It appears that parents and educators have approached Dewey and his philosophy in three different ways. Some have stopped before reaching Dewey, assuming without examination that the man is "bad" and should not be read, let alone followed. Others have gone right past Dewey never stopping to examine his ideas; they have emerged with what they believe is truly "progressive" education, although actually their ideas are in no way related to Dewey. Not too many have gone through Dewey's writings, examining his ideas in light of present conditions, judging their worth, and reconstructing new programs in teaching that in part accept and in part modify Dewey's conceptions.

Any hope for the intelligent improvement of educational practice seems to rest with the third approach. Much of what Dewey advocated has not been realized. In large part, our schools have been pouring new wines into old bottles. Only snatches of Dewey's ideas have crept into the schools. Nor are the schools entirely at fault. Dewey's educational program is a fantastically difficult one to realize—certainly it cannot come about in one or even two generations. The philosopher's plan involved far more than simply installing moveable furniture or having people sit in circles. In his scheme of things, an entire climate emerges—a democratic climate. We lose sight of the purpose of our schools when we think that our only mission is to teach people more and more factual knowledge in the best possible way. Fascist and communist societies also teach facts—and very effectively. What we must also remember is that we are trying to educate people for a way of life and in a manner that reflects this way of life. Facts alone will never make men free. Nor can a society that creates an exclusive elite of the intelligent claim to be democratic. Here is the soul of Dewey's entire philosophy: a system of education that best recognizes the dignity and worth of all individuals, that allows every individual to develop to his fullest, and that teaches the virtues of democracy by establishing a democratic atmosphere.

Finally, Dewey needs to be corrected and modified. If Dewey were to be resurrected, he undoubtedly would be the first man to criticize his own ideas. His metaphysical foundation, the idea that we live in a dynamic world where conditions and ideas change, would compel him to do so. Dewey, at the turn of the century, could not foresee an atomic age, which, with all its promised goodness, also has accentuated the anxiety of young people about tomorrow. Dewey did not make explicit the differences in the different levels of learning. Children learn as children, but adolescents have different interests and different problems, and similarly, adults cannot be taught the same way we teach children. There cannot be one method that will resolve the problems of "education." Each level needs to work out its own way of teaching. Equally important, each school needs to understand its students' uniqueness and create a proper educational program for *that* school and in *that* time.

Dewey remains a seminal figure in the history of modern educational thought. He brought forth new ways to solve old problems. He, more than any other man, brought democracy and education to a systematic unity. He remains a great thinker to be read, understood, and modified.

John Dewey: Educator of Nations

By WILLIAM W. BRICKMAN

FOR OVER HALF A CENTURY, educators of six continents have been acknowledging the contributions of John Dewey to educational thought and practice in their countries.[1] As far back as 1882, at the age of 23, his name was first mentioned in a foreign journal, the *Revue Philosophique* of France, in relation to an abstract of his first published article which had appeared the year before in the *Journal of Speculative Philosophy*. It was not until 1899, apparently, that his educational ideas were discussed in European publications. The occasion was an article by the renowned French scholar, Gabriel Compayré, in "La Grande Encyclopédie." Evidently, Compayré, and other European educators as well, read Dewey's educational writings in English.

So far as the present writer has been able to determine, the first foreign edition of a Dewey work in the field of education was "The School and Society," which was issued in London in 1900, only one year after its publication in the United States. It is likewise very probable that the first translation of a Deweyan pedagogical work was into Swedish in 1900 ("Interest as Related to Will").

Other writings by Dewey were rendered into various languages and his name became quite

[1] For documentation, see William W. Brickman, "John Dewey's Foreign Reputation as an Educator," *School and Society*, 70: 257-265, Oct. 22, 1949. Some of the recent references were obtained through the courtesy of W. A. Mustakim, Education Clearing House, Unesco, Paris.

well known in pedagogical circles in Europe prior to World War I. The spirit of postwar reform, which also affected education, was responsible for the spreading of Dewey's doctrines to other parts of the world.

That Dewey's thinking about education won adherents in Europe, Asia, and other areas was quite a phenomenon, since Americans, as a general rule, were not deemed worthy of serious consideration in cultural, intellectual, and educational circles. Dewey's views on education became known at a time when fresh pedagogical winds were blowing across Europe. Pestalozzi, Herbart, and Froebel had had their heyday, and new stars were appearing. The new socio-economic and political movements at the turn of the century and thereafter demanded different educational content, principles, and practices. The newcomers, preaching a breakaway from classical subjects, the adoption of activistic procedures, and a stress on scientific and social subjects, restated many 19th-century ideas on education. The New School Movement in England, Germany, France, and other countries made educators familiar with modern concepts which paved the way for Dewey's thought. Possibly because Dewey seldom mentioned or quoted from Pestalozzi and the other great educators of the recent past, many a European educator may have felt that there was something new in the writings of the American pedagogue. As time went on, Dewey's writings were increasingly mentioned for the purpose of supporting the views of foreign educators.

Prof. J. J. Findlay of the University of Manchester was probably the first to direct the attention of the British pedagogical public to Dewey. The two volumes of Deweyan writings which he edited in 1907 and 1910 were widely circulated. In the second of these books, "Educational Essays," Findlay referred to "the gospel according to John Dewey." Among Dewey's works published in England were "The School and Society" (second edition, 1915) and "Schools of Tomorrow." The volume by Katherine C. Mayhew and Anna C. Edwards, "The Dewey School," also was issued in a British edition. Since there was no language problem, British educators could often get to read the original editions as printed in America.

Chapters on Dewey were included in several important educational works by British writers, such as W. J. McCallister's "The Growth of Freedom in Education" (1931). Interestingly enough, the second edition of Robert R. Rusk's classic, "The Doctrines of The Great Educators" (1954), added a sizable chapter on Dewey. Dr. Rusk, a Scotsman, declared that Dewey "dominated the educational stage . . . throughout the first half of the twentieth century" as did Pestalozzi a century earlier.

Most recently, "A Short History of Educational Ideas" (1956), by S. J. Curtis and M. E. A. Boultwood, devoted one of its longest chapters to the life, work, and impact of John Dewey. The authors are appreciative, but they also cite the leading critics and their views.

Dewey's fortunes in Great Britain are hard to assess. Sir Percy Nunn, in a frequently quoted remark, stated that Dewey "did much to emancipate the professional intelligence of the present generation of teachers." Even though, as Curtis and Boultwood say, Dewey was recognized in England "as a leader in educational thought by the time of the First World War," he did not gain recognition in all leading circles. In John Adams'

"The Evolution of Educational Theory" (1912), for instance, there are discussions of the ideas of Herman H. Horne, William C. Bagley, Edward L. Thorndike, and other American educators, but Dewey is not even mentioned.

Dewey's name and ideas are as likely to be found in British works on education as they are to be omitted, depending on the nature of the writer's viewpoint. Those who draw inspiration from the religious and the classical worlds seldom refer to him. Of late, there seems to have developed a tendency to look upon Dewey less as a pedagogical deity than as an important thinker whose ideas were neither to be accepted nor rejected *in toto*. Typical of this is the appraisal in the chapter on pragmatism by A. V. Judges of King's College, University of London, in the book he edited in 1957, "Education and the Philosophic Mind." Prof. Judges, who describes himself as a student of Dewey, was attracted by "his robust belief that high intelligence in the pupil, and its capacity for employment towards large and good, though indefinable ends, are the reward of the sound teacher" (p. 100). On the other hand, "that honest, lumbering, and infelicitous style of Dewey's which seldom offers a vivid and clear-cut picture of anything, helped to conceal the inadequacy of the pragmatic argument to maintain the position of an earnest radical of the great liberal tradition" *(ibid.)*.

It was not until 1909 when some of Dewey's educational writings were published in France. Georges Bertier, the leader of Ecole Nouvelle Movement, issued in *L'Education* a partial translation of "The School and Society" that year and three years later. In 1925, the famous Belgian educator, Ovide Decroly, translated "How We

Think" for a French publishing company, which also issued six years later a translation of "Schools of Tomorrow." French publications by or on Dewey have been rather widely spaced, with "Experience and Education" appearing in 1947 and "Freedom and Culture" in 1957. The former also contained an exposition of Dewey's pedagogical ideas by the translator, A. Carroi.

French monographs on John Dewey also seem to be scarce. A Chinese instructor of philosophy, Ou Tsuin-Chen, obtained in 1931 a *doctorat-ès-lettres* from the Sorbonne for his thesis, "La doctrine pedagogique de John Dewey," which included a translation of "My Pedagogic Creed." This author claimed that there did not exist any systematic treatment of Dewey's pedagogy in France. Evidently, he did not think much of his fellow-countryman's earlier doctoral dissertation at the University of Lyon, Jyan Choy's (Tsai Yang) "Etude comparative sur les doctrines pédagogiques de Durkheim et de Dewey" (1926), or of the doctoral dissertation of Nelson J. Crowell, "John Dewey et l'éducation nouvelle" (1928), at the University of Lausanne, Switzerland. Incidentally, Tsuin-Chen overestimated the French educators' appreciation of Dewey. Perhaps the best of the published dissertations in French on Dewey was "John Dewey Educateur" (1932), presented by Reuben Wallenrod, now at Brooklyn College, to the Sorbonne.

In recent years, the French seemed to have kept up an interest in Dewey's educational thought, to judge from such a volume as M.-A. Bloch's "Philosophie de l'éducation nouvelle" (1948); the publication of "L'oeuvre de John Dewey" (1955), by the Comité Français pour l'éducation préscolaire of Pantin; and the inclusion of a chapter by John S. Brubacher in

"Les grands pédagogues," edited by Jean Chateau (1956). On the whole, however, it would appear that, over the decades, Dewey was more honored in France for his philosophy than for his education.

First Edouard Claparède and then Adolphe Ferrière brought Dewey to the attention of the pedagogues of Switzerland. The former, a renowned child psychologist, began discussing Dewey as early as 1905 in his writings, but his introduction to Pidoux's translation of four essays by Dewey (1913) laid the groundwork for the Swiss appreciation of the American educator. The only other Swiss translation of a Dewey book that the writer could locate was one in German of "How We Think" (1951). Possibly, the polyglot Swiss educators have done their reading of Dewey in the translations published in Germany and France or else in English. It is apparent that the thesis by Crowell, cited in an earlier paragraph, was the only Swiss publication of more than article size on Dewey.

In 1949, the writer stated that "few of Dewey's educational writings appear to be available in Italian." The two educational works by Dewey in Italian translation, the periodical references, the occasional monograph, and the treatment in a pedagogical book were the sum total of his educational reputation in Italy during the Fascist era and in the early post-World War II years. It is possible that the presence of Carleton Washburne in Italy as a military government officer in the field of education may have given an impetus to Italian interest in Dewey. Since about 1948, seldom has a year passed when at least one translation of a philosophical or educational work by Dewey did not appear. Among the translated educational volumes were "Democracy and

Education" (in 1949 and again in 1951), "The School and Society" (1949, 1954), and "Education Today" (1950). A further indication of the importance of Dewey for Italian pedagogy is the appearance of six monographs between 1950 and 1957 on his educational thought. One of these, Gino Corallo's "La pedagogia di Giovanni Dewey" (1950) is a tome of more than 600 pages, including a comprehensive bibliography of writings by and about Dewey. Another, Lamberto Borghi's "John Dewey e il pensiero pedagogico contemporaneo negli Stati Uniti" (1951), is a scholarly analysis of Dewey's impact on American educational thought, and it is too bad that it has not been translated as yet into English. Mention also should be made of Ernesto Codignola, whose books contain numerous discussions of Dewey and who has translated and otherwise publicized the American educator in Italy.

In Spain, Domingo Barnés, secretary of the Museo Pedagógico Nacional, translated "The School and Society" in 1915 (second edition, 1929), and several years later Lorenzo Luzuriaga began writing on Dewey's theories and translating many of his pedagogical works. During the 1920's, at least nine translations appeared in Spain, with additional ones being published in the early 1930's. The eight volumes of the collected "Obras pedagógicas" were issued in Madrid, probably during the half-decade prior to the Spanish Civil War. With the coming of the conflict, Prof. Luzuriaga fled to Argentina and continued his Dewey translations and other pedagogical writing. Apart from these educators, few Spanish educators seem to have devoted attention to Dewey, particularly during the Franco period. It was a rare Spanish writer who acknowledged Dewey's educational leadership in the past two decades.

The pedagogical ideas of Dewey were brought before the German educators by Lucinda P. Boggs, an American, who wrote a Ph.D. thesis in German in 1901 on the application of Dewey's theory of interest to pedagogy. Then came some translations, but mainly a large number of discussions and references in encyclopedias, books, and pedagogical periodicals. The chief translator was Prof. Erich Hylla, who first rendered "Democracy and Education" into German in 1930 and then published a second edition in 1949.

The educator who was largely responsible for the growth of Dewey's reputation in Germany was Georg Kerschensteiner, who himself was becoming world-famous. The German pedagogue, interestingly enough, learned first about Dewey in 1907 from an English edition of "The School and Society" rather than from Elsa Gurlitt's German translation (1905). Until his death a quarter of a century later, Kerschensteiner did much to spread Dewey's thought through his many influential writings. Even if one discounts the claims by some writers that Dewey exerted a strong influence on Kerschensteiner, it is still evident that the American was more than a source of mere inspiration to the German educator.

The outstanding individual to insist that Kerschensteiner drew heavily upon Dewey is the Belgian priest, Franz De Hovre, whose original Flemish writings are better known in French and English translation. In spite of his criticism of Dewey in "Philosophy and Education" as "a rather biased social educator" (p. 115) who is silent about the cultural bases of society and religious belief, Father De Hovre regards him as "one of the leading philosophers and educators of our day" (p. 114). Apart from pointing up Dewey's influence in Germany, De Hovre feels that the American educator also was influential in England.

The Dutch pedagogical profession showed some interest in Dewey's work, as evidenced by references and discussions in various educational writings. However, there seems to have been but one translation, "The School and Society," in 1929. The celebrated Dutch pedagogue, Jan Lighthart, respected Dewey and noted similarities between the thinking of the two, but there does not appear to be any clear-cut proof that the American influenced him to any extent.

Swedish awareness of Dewey as an educator dates at least from 1901, when "Interest as Related to Will" was published in translation. This interest was shown over the years through additional translations, at least one significant critical monograph, and miscellaneous mentions in various pedagogical publications. In 1948, "Democracy and Education" was issued in Swedish.

The other Scandinavian countries evidently have paid little special attention to Dewey, for one reason or another. An exception is the scholarly volume (1953) in which a Norwegian educator, Sigurd Nørstebø evaluated Dewey's educational theory.

The reputation of Dewey in Russia is discussed by the writer at greater length in the following chapter. It can be traced to Stanislav T. Shatski, one of the greatest Russian pedagogues, who became familiar with Dewey's ideas by 1905. Russian translations of Dewey's writings appear as early as 1907, with most of them being published in the 1920's, when his fame in the Soviet Union was at its zenith. Dewey visited

Soviet Russia in 1928 and was received enthusiastically. However, the change in Soviet educational policy in 1931 resulted in the dropping of Dewey's doctrines, and in the years after World War II the American educator has been branded as a "reactionary," "imperialist," and "warmonger."

The Slavic countries were quite interested in the work and writings of Dewey. Translations and monographs were published in Poland, Czechoslovakia, Bulgaria, and Yugoslavia. By printing in 1956 a translation of "How We Think," the Polish educators showed the possibility of breaking through the Iron Curtain, so far as Dewey is concerned.

There is evidence that Dewey has been translated in Austria, Romania, Hungary, Greece, and Turkey. His ideas have been described and mentioned in the educational works of Portugal, Denmark, and Finland. Dewey was invited by the Turkish government in 1924 to visit its schools and to sum up his impressions. The report was printed in Turkish as "Türkiye maarifi hakkinda rapor" and was reprinted as recently as 1952. This may be an indication of the continuing interest in that country in Deweyan ideas. The writer has attempted, while in Turkey and subsequently, to obtain a copy of Dewey's original English report but has not been successful thus far.

During the past decade, translations of Dewey's writings were issued in India, China (Taiwan), Korea, and Egypt. The Hebrew University, Jerusalem, Israel, has named its School of Education after John Dewey. But it remained for Japan to take to Dewey after World War II, as China had done following World War I. Since 1950, at least 10 translations of the Deweyan works, philosophical and educational, were published in Japanese. And while there is some reaction against Dewey in Japanese educational circles, as there was in pre-Communist China and currently in the United States, many Japanese educators seem attached to Dewey's pedagogy. The recently formed John Dewey Society in Japan has a large number of philosophers as members. The name of Dewey has penetrated into Africa from north to south, in part because of the influence of the educators from the various regions who had studied about him in the United States and Europe.

Although Dewey's work is well known all over Central and South America, only in three countries is there an active interest in his thought. In Mexico the interest has been mainly philosophical; in Brazil it has been both philosophical and educational; and in Argentina, chiefly educational. Prof. Lorenzo Luzuriaga of the University of Buenos Aires, a prolific writer on modern education, has translated at least six of Dewey's books during the past two decades.

Canadian awareness of Dewey's educational work goes back, according to Charles E. Phillips' recent history of Canadian education, to 1899. Between the wars, many of his ideas were put into practice and many a Canadian educator has testified to the impact of Dewey on education in his country. Even a severe critic, such as Hilda Neatby, who can match denunciations with any American counterpart, has admitted that Dewey's teachings "have had an incalculable influence on Canadian education."

Without going into details, it can be shown that Dewey's fame also reached down into New Zealand and Australia as well as into various areas in Southeast Asia. There are writings on

Dewey, including translations, in such languages as Armenian and Yiddish. It is not too much to say that few educators have enjoyed so extensive a reputation as did—and does—Dewey.

Very possibly, this world-wide reputation of Dewey is not without its shady side. Perhaps too many countries took too much too soon from his doctrines without enough reflection on the relationship of Deweyan thought to their own traditions. Some countries have had second thoughts about the desirability of continuing to follow the American's educational leadership. Certain it is that most nations drawing upon Dewey did so out of the pressing necessity to reform their school systems at once. Dewey's ideas and practice appeared to show the way and they consequently were adopted.

In many countries which the writer has visited, there are numerous educators who seem to be unaware of any other American pedagogical thinker save Dewey or that ideas similar to his can be found in their own history. This is unfortunate, but it does indicate the depth of Dewey's reputation.

Dewey's educational work is known all over the world. In some areas his views have brought about changes in educational philosophy and practice. There is a reaction against Dewey in some sections and it may continue for some time to come. The influence of John Dewey may wane or it may even be strengthened. At any rate it is doubtful if the record of his universal repute can be erased—or, perhaps, even matched.

Dewey and Russia[1]

By WILLIAM W. BRICKMAN

JOHN DEWEY first became known in Russia, apparently, when Alexander Zelenko, a Russian engineer who lived during 1903-04 at Hull House in Chicago, returned to Moscow and spread the Hull House idea. Among those who learned about Jane Addams—and very probably Dewey —was the noted educator, Stanislav T. Shatski. As early as 1907, "The School and Society" appeared in Russian.

The 1917 revolution popularized Dewey's ideas. During the 1920's, several Russian translations of "School of Tomorrow," "The School and Society," and other works were published. Shatski, Pavel P. Blonski, Albert P. Pinkevitch, Anatol Lunacharski, and other early Soviet educators frequently mentioned Dewey and used his ideas. Thus, Pinkevitch valued Dewey's thinking despite the American's non-Marxian orientation, and he urged all students of education to study Dewey's works. He regarded Dewey as the foreign thinker closest to the spirit of Marxism and Russian Communism—lavish praise, indeed, from the Soviet viewpoint.

Dewey visited Russia in 1928 as a member of a 25-man American delegation. His "Impressions of Soviet Russia" were sympathetic enough to earn him the label of "Bolshevik" in some American newspapers. However, he observed that, according to Communist educators, "propaganda is education and education is propaganda."

---

[1] Condensed from a lecture, Oct. 8, 1959, Southern Illinois University, Carbondale. The documented lecture may be published in book form.

Moreover, propaganda and education "are more than confounded; they are identified by the Soviet pedagogues." He did appreciate the achievements of the Soviet schools, expressing his amazement "at the progress already made." The Soviet school system was "a going concern; a self-moving organism."

In 1931, the "Bolshaya Sovetskaya Entsiklopediya" described Dewey as "an outstanding American philosopher, psychologist, sociologist, and pedagogue" (Vol. 23, pp. 717-720) and presented his ideas in a long article. In the same year, however, the Communist Party of the Soviet Union decided to get rid of all Progressive educational practices and Dewey's star began to drop. Four years later, Pinkevitch, who had lauded Dewey, mentioned his name only once in his "Science and Education in the U.S.S.R." As the years went on, the de-Deweyization of Soviet education proceeded at a rapid pace, but the name of Dewey was evidently still respected. The Trotsky Inquiry, under the chairmanship of Dewey, which resulted in the exoneration of Stalin's opponent, led to the condemnation of Dewey by the U.S.S.R. and by Communists all over the world. Despite all this, Dewey was still given reasonable attention in E. N. Medynskii's "Istoria Pedagogiki" (Moscow, 1941, Vol. I).

Since the Cold War began, there seems to have developed a strong movement in the Soviet Union to attack Dewey personally as well as professionally. The "Bolshaya Sovetskaya Entsiklopediya," in its 1952 edition, cut down the size of the article on Dewey. Here he is described as "a reactionary bourgeois philosopher and sociologist" who worked "in the interests of the aggressive policy of the government of the U.S.A." Moreover, Dewey is charged with "spreading racial obscurantism, amorality, unscrupulousness." He also is condemned for using education as a tool to indoctrinate capitalism on the one hand and to foment hatred of Communism on the other. The article concludes: "The philosophy of Dewey is the philosophy of war and fascism. Dewey is the proclaimer of contemporary American reaction, an ideologist of American imperialism, [and] a violent enemy of the U.S.S.R., the country of the people's democracy and of the revolutionary theory of Marxism- Leninism." This was a typical Soviet judgment.

According to the experts of the Academy of Pedagogical Sciences in Moscow, the best example of a recent research study on the history of educational thought is a monograph on Dewey: "Pedagogika D. Diui na sluzhbe sovremennoi Amerikanskoi reaktsii" ("The Pedagogy of J. Dewey in the Service of Contemporary American Reaction"), by V. S. Shevkin (1952).[2] The first chapter contains footnote references to Lenin, Marx and Engels, Stalin, Zhdanov, Kalinin, and Malenkov, and to only one educator, Herbart, but no reference to Dewey's writings. The second chapter is entitled "Pragmatism—Instrumentalism—the Philosophical Foundation of the Reactionary Pedagogy." While it is a critique of the doctrines of William James and John Dewey, its documentation is loaded with citations from the works of Marx, Lenin, Stalin, and their followers. The third chaper is "The Pseudoscientific Meaning of Pragmatic Pedagogy"; and the fifth and final chapter, "J. Dewey, the Henchman of Contemporary Imperialist Reaction." There are references to Dewey's writings, but his ideas are

---

[2] A portion of the book was published in 1955 in East Germany: "Die Pädagogik J. Deweys" (Berlin: Volk und Wissen Verlag).

appraised in accordance with the principles of Marxism-Leninism-Stalinism.

In the final chapter, Shevkin concludes that "Dewey is the wicked enemy not only of the American people but also of all the freedom-loving peoples on our earth. The entire system of his views on the world, society, and the younger generation is, knowing no bounds, an apologetic for American imperialism" (p. 135, translation by the present writer). On the other hand, Prof. Shevkin presents as a true educator "the great leader of the Soviet people and of all progressive mankind, I. V. Stalin" (*ibid.*, p. 142).

Such is the general account of the decline of Dewey's doctrines in the Soviet Union. He may be highly respected all over the world, even in the United States and Poland, but nowhere has he been dragged down, defamed, and denigrated as he has been in the land of Lenin, Stalin, and Khrushchev.

Dewey's Letters, 1894-1904:

A PRELIMINARY LISTING
By ROBERT L. McCAUL

Although it is now a century since his birth, a full-scale, interpretative biography of John Dewey has yet to be written. For Dewey, more perhaps than for any recent philosopher, such a biography would be of especial value because he needed contact with people and things to give his ideas vitality and concrete significance. Of his own development he said: "Upon the whole, the forces that have influenced me have come from persons and situations more than from books—not that I have not, I hope, learned a great deal from philosophical writings, but that what I have learned from them has been technical in comparison with what I have been forced to think upon and about because of some experience in which I found myself entangled."[2]

Granted the value of a biography which would relate the influence of persons, situations, and

---

[1] I wish to express my appreciation for assistance received from Mrs. Mary G. Cary, curator of the Swarthmore College Peace Collection, and from Mrs. Herbert A. Kellar, co-ordinator of the McCormick Collection of the State Historical Society of Wisconsin, and for permission to include materials from these collections in my list. I also wish to thank Robert Rosenthal and Roland Dickson, Department of Special Collections, Harper Library, University of Chicago, and Prof. Richard J. Storr of the University of Chicago and his research assistant, Ruth Necheles, for their help.

[2] In G. P. Adams and W. P. Montague, editors, "Contemporary American Philosophy," Vol. 2 (New York: Macmillan, 1930), p. 22.

experiences to the development of Dewey's thought, the first obstacle is that of gathering the primary materials upon which a biography should be based. Dewey's articles and books in print are listed in M. Halsey Thomas' "A Bibliography of John Dewey, 1882-1939" (New York: Columbia University Press, 1939). No comparable calendar of Dewey's unpublished work or of his voluminous private and official correspondence exists. He exchanged letters with many persons; he belonged to many institutions and organizations; he worked for many political, social, and educational causes. All the correspondence related to these activities is scattered here and there, in bulk or in part unknown and unappraised. To find and make an inventory of even that portion located in one place is, as I can testify, an exceedingly time consuming and frustrating chore. But we must break trail for Dewey's future biographer. Perhaps publication of this annotated list of materials will encourage other institutions and other persons to make known what they have of Dewey's.

The 143 items listed chronologically here begin with Dewey's letter of Feb. 15, 1894, optimistically viewing the opportunities in prospect at the University of Chicago, and end with his letter of June 16, 1904, after he angrily had resigned from the university and was about to move to Columbia and New York. By and large, the letters over the 10-year Chicago period relate more directly to the evolution of Dewey's educational ideas than to the development of his philosophical thought. Many of the letters deal with his administrative activities as head professor of the Department of Philosophy and Department of Pedagogy and as director of the School of Education. These expose his thinking on pedagogy as a university discipline and teacher training as a university function and on the proper role of an organizational unit devoted to educational study, teaching, and research within an embracing university framework. Other items deal with the purpose, operation, and financing of the Dewey School (the Laboratory School); others with the vicissitudes of his relations with Harper, Mrs. Emmons Blaine, and with the Parker faculty after the Parker-Blaine teacher training institute had been absorbed by the university.

To pass judgment on the importance of these letters is impossible, of course, for "importance" is a variable that fluctuates with the nature of the problem or hypothesis that the investigator brings to the material. Nevertheless, it can be said with assurance that the period from 1894 to 1904, when Dewey was on the faculty of the University of Chicago, was an exceedingly important one in his development. During the decade he completed his movement from absolutism to relativism, from idealism to naturalism, from Hegelianism to experimentalism, from formal logic to instrumental logic, and from an analytic psychology to a functional psychology. In his famous Laboratory School, he tested his ideas and worked out their educational bearings, and he found in education a focus which enabled him to fuse these ideas into operative unity.

In the following list the two letters to Jane Addams are in the Swarthmore College Peace Collection, Swarthmore, Pa., and all of the letters to Mrs. Emmons Blaine are in the McCormick Collection of the State Historical Society of Wisconsin at Madison. The rest of the materials are in the archives of the William

Rainey Harper Memorial Library of the University of Chicago. Other letters than those listed are extant, I am sure, and that is why this listing of Dewey's letters is labelled "preliminary." For example, M. Halsey Thomas, curator of Columbiana, Columbia University, tells me that in the Low Memorial Library there is some Dewey correspondence from the Chicago years. Then there are a few letters reproduced in Vol. 2 of Ralph Barton Perry's "The Thought and Character of William James" (Boston: Little, Brown, 1935). The Swarthmore, Wisconsin, Chicago, Columbia, and Harvard holdings may provide scholars with a fairly representative sampling of Dewey correspondence between 1894 and 1904, though how close to a complete run no one yet can tell.

DEWEY LETTERS

1. To Harper, Feb. 15, 1894. Written. 2pp. Regards certain features of Chicago proposal as "appealing," but salary offered seems inadequate.

2. To Harper, March 19, 1894. Written. 1p. Is happy to receive news of his appointment, for "a great chance exists and I hope to be able to improve it." Will resign his professorship at University of Michigan, as of July 1.

3. To Harper, Oct. 19, 1895. Written. 3pp. Lists the needs for additional faculty and money for psychological laboratory, publications, and fellowships.

4. To editor, *Chicago Evening Post*, Dec. 19, 1895. Newspaper clipping. Argues that Chicago Board of Education should accept the gift of the Cook County Normal School [the Parker Training School].

5. To Harper, Jan. 11, 1896. Typed. 2pp. Answers criticisms of Dewey School by Julia E. Bulkley, associate professor of pedagogy.

6. To Jane Addams, Jan. 19, 1896. Written. 2pp. Praises her "Pullman paper" and suggests a few stylistic changes.

7. To Harper, Feb. 1, 1896. Written. 1p. Says Charles H. Thurber, associate professor of pedagogy, should be able to offer courses, especially in secondary education and in administration and organization, of distinct advantage to department.

8. To [Board of Trustees], no date [probably spring, 1896]. Typed. 4pp. Shows relation between experimental school and theoretical instruction in pedagogy and asks for funds for Dewey School.

9. To Harper, Oct. 23, 1896. Written. 1p. Thinks student record form should be simplified.

10. To Harper, Nov. 12, 1896. Written. 1p. Reports that Hibbard, Spencer, and Bartlett Co. has given tools for carpenter shop to Dewey School.

11. To Henry A. Rust, comptroller, Nov. 12, 1896. Written. 1p. Similar to the preceding.

12. To Harper, Nov. 18, 1896. Typed. 1p. Suggests need for more uniformity among departments in expectations of service from fellows and other students getting financial assistance.

13. To T. W. Goodspeed, secretary of the Board of Trustees, Nov. 23, 1896. Typed. 2pp. Statement of budget of Dewey School for 1896-97.

14. To Board of Libraries, Dec. 7, 1896. Typed. 3pp. Proposes principles for more effectively dividing funds and books between central and departmental libraries.

15. To Harper, Dec. 9, 1896. Typed. 1p. Wishes to talk to Harper about possibility of university's giving land on which to erect a building for Dewey School.

16. To Harper, Jan. 8, 1897. Typed. 1p. Encloses statement [next item] about a fully equipped Department of Pedagogy and also a reprint of his article, "Pedagogy as a University Discipline," *University Record*, 1:353-355, 361-363.

17. Enclosure with letter to Harper, Jan. 8, 1897. *Plan for Organization of Work in a Fully Equipped Department of Pedagogy.* Typed. 7pp. Describes lines of work included within the scope of a University Department of Pedagogy.

18. To Mrs. Emmons Blaine, Jan. 8, 1897. Typed. 1p. Is sending her materials about Dewey School and invites her to visit.

19. To Harper, Jan. 11, 1897. Typed. 1p. Asks if the university physician may be called on to examine Dewey School children.

20. To Harper, Jan. 14, 1897. Typed. 1p. Says arrangements made for dancing class for Dewey School children; inquires whether free tickets to Art Institute available for teachers and children.

21. To William D. MacClintock, associate professor of English, Feb. 2, 1897. Typed. 1p. Says he must postpone decision on hiring an instructor in aesthetics until he has consulted members of his department.

22. To MacClintock, Feb. 3, 1897. Typed. 1p. Recognizes desirability of having more courses in aesthetics, but has no money in budget.

23. To Harper, Feb. 23, 1897. Typed. 1p. Finds Julia Bulkley's plan of her course in modern German Pedagogy somewhat vague.

24. To Harper, March 20, 1897. Typed. 1p. Agrees that it would be desirable to unite elementary and secondary school conferences.

25. To Harper, April 28, 1897. Typed. 1p. Wishes to do all he can to hold George H. Locke, who has received an offer from Harvard.

26. To Harper, April 28, 1897. Typed. 1p. Would approve appointment of Edward S. Ames, but department is more in need of someone to teach experimental psychology.

27. To Harper, May 13, 1897. Typed. 3pp. Summarizes James R. Angell's report on the work in experimental psychology.

28. To Goodspeed, secretary, Committee on Expenditures, Board of Trustees, no date [probably autumn, 1897]. Written. 1p. Sample Department of Philosophy letterhead attached. Lists supplies needed for library and office of the department.

29. To Harper, Nov. 8, 1897. Typed. 1p. Reports gifts to Dewey School for support of music and purchase of pictures and statuary.

30. To Harper, Dec. 6, 1897. Typed. 2pp. States points that should be considered in planning a joint effort by the Department of Pedagogy and other departments in preparing secondary school teachers.

31. To Harper, Dec. 6, 1897. Typed. 5pp. Outlines faculty-personnel needs of the Department of Pedagogy, now at a critical stage in its existence.

32. To Harper, Jan. 4, 1898. Typed. 2pp. Suggests pedagogical subjects appropriate for graduate student and faculty assemblies; volunteers to talk on pedagogics of college teaching.

33. To Harper, Feb. 9, 1898. Typed. 1p. Has engaged Charles McMurry to teach in first term of summer and hopes to get McLennan of Oberlin to give work in child study.

34. To Harper, March 1, 1898. Typed. 1p. Mentions persons (Ames, Wilbur Jackman, Ella Flagg Young) who may teach philosophy or pedagogy courses.

35. To Harper, April 5, 1898. Typed. 1p. Statement of anticipated expenditures on salaries for summer pedagogy staff.

36. To Harper, April 12, 1898. Typed. 1p. Speaks of need for an assistant in experimental psychology in summer.

37. To Harper, May 11, 1898. Typed. 1p. Has made no plans for an elementary school conference this year.

38. To Harper, June 23, 1898. Typed. 4pp. Opposes

Harper's suggestion that Dewey School tuition be raised and size of classes be increased.

39. To Jane Addams, Oct. 12, 1898. Written. 1p. Agrees that "the assumption that there is or may be antagonism is bad," and is glad he found this out before talking on social psychology.

40. To Harper, Dec. 23, 1898. Written. 1p. Suggests S. S. Laurie and Sir Joshua Fitch as possible "stars" for summer quarter.

41. To Harper, Jan. 16, 1899. Typed. 1p. Reports gift to Dewey School of $20 from R. R. Whitehead, Santa Barbara.

42. To Harper, Feb. 10, 1899. Typed. 1p. Believes "Department of Education" a better title than "Department of Pedagogy" or "Department of the Science and Art of Education."

43. To Harper, March 6, 1899. Typed. 1p. Reports gift of $200 to Dewey School and confesses he finds it difficult to answer questions as to why school is not supported out of university funds.

44. To Harper, March 8, 1899. Typed. 2pp. Feels that it is time for the Board of Trustees to indicate definitely their whole attitude toward the Dewey School.

45. To Mrs. Blaine, March 22, 1899. Written. 1p. Sending course announcements and tickets for herself and other persons who might be interested.

46. To Mrs. Blaine, Nov. 1, 1899. Written. 1p. Thanks her for her "very great generosity which made possible the publication of the lectures I gave last year" ["The School and Society"].

47. To Harper, Nov. 16, 1899. Written. 1p. Thinks that proposed action by the dean would cause Ella Flagg Young to sever relations with university.

48. To Harper, Dec. 6, 1899. Typed. 1p. Reports gift of two typewriters to Dewey School from William Kent, Chicago.

49. To Harper, Dec. 21, 1899. Typed. 5pp. Presents recommendations with reference to philosophy and pedagogy budget for 1900-01.

50. To Harper, Dec. 21, 1899. Typed. 1p. Reports gifts to Dewey School of $1,000 from Miss Mary Castle, Honolulu, and Mrs. William R. Linn, Chicago.

51. To Harper, Jan. 11, 1900. Typed. 1p. Reports gift to Dewey School of dishes from J. W. Brooks, Chicago.

52. To Harper, Jan. 18, 1900. Typed. 1p. Reports gift to Dewey School of $1,000 from Miss Mary Castle.

53. To Harper, Jan. 23, 1900. Typed. 1p. Reports gift to Dewey School of a hand-power circular rip saw from A. C. Bartlett, Chicago.

54. To Mrs. Blaine, Jan. 25, 1900. Written. 1p. Will

be glad to meet her and trustees of the Chicago [Parker-Blaine] Institute, as she requests.

55. To Harper, Jan. 30, 1900. Written on bottom of a note from Harper. 1p. Ames could give work in the history of philosophy next summer.

56. To Harper, Feb. 3, 1900. Typed. 4pp. Suggests additions to faculty of Departments of Philosophy and Pedagogy and to staff of Dewey School.

57. To Mrs. Blaine, Feb. 27, 1900. Written. 1p. Has sent her a copy of the new edition of "The School and Society" and would be happy to send more.

58. To Mrs. Blaine, March 14, 1900. Written. 1p. Wishes to call her attention to an exhibit of water colors by an artist who is a friend of the Deweys.

59. To Press Department, June 12, 1900. Typed. 1p. Because of University of Chicago Press's slowness in bringing out a new edition of "The School and Society," has proposed to McClure Co. that they take over the book.

60. To Harper, June 28, 1900. Written. 1p. Has asked McClure Co. for release from arrangement he had made with them, though he feels that his agreement with University of Chicago Press to publish "The School and Society" was terminable at the pleasure of either party.

61. To Mrs. Blaine, July 19 [1900]. Written. 1p. Is at Chautauqua; Mrs. Dewey[3] is in Chicago, having just given birth to a girl, and may join him and the other children.

62. To Mrs. Blaine, July 19, 1900. Telegram. Until he hears from Mrs. Dewey, cannot give definite answer to request to come to Chicago to advise trustees of Chicago Institute.

63. To Mrs. Blaine, July 20 [1900]. Written. 1p. "I wonder if I knew the special points on which you want my judgment whether I could not be of about as much use in giving it in written form."

64. To Mrs. Blaine, July 20, 1900. Telegram. Can't he advise her and trustees by correspondence?

65. To Mrs. Blaine, July 21 [1900]. Written. 1p. Cannot answer her request until he knows Mrs. Dewey's plans.

66. To Mrs. Blaine, July 21, 1900. Telegram. Cannot answer until he gets home.

67. To Mrs. Blaine, July 23 [1900]. Telegram. Will meet her at any convenient place and hour.

68. To Mrs. Blaine, Aug. 2, 1900. Written. 2pp. Lists seven suggestions for improving physical layout of new school being planned by institute trustees.

69. To Mrs. Blaine, Aug. 22, 1900. Written. 1p. Wants no remuneration for his suggestions and wishes them to be taken as evidence of his interest in the project.

---

[3] The Mrs. Dewey referred to in these letters is, of course, the late Alice Chipman Dewey and not the present Mrs. Roberta Grant Dewey.

70. To Goodspeed, Dec. 18, 1900. Written. 1p. Encloses Mr. J. R. Campbell's pledge to give $50 per annum to Dewey School.

71. To Harper, Feb. 16, 1901. Typed. 1p. Lists courses in the Department of Pedagogy that Pres. Nathaniel Butler, Colby University, might give in summer at University of Chicago.

72. To Butler, Feb. 16, 1901. Typed. 1p. If Butler leaves Colby and comes to University of Chicago to work with co-operating schools, he is welcome to give courses in educational philosophy or the history of education.

73. To Francis W. Parker, director, School of Education, May 29, 1901. Typed. 1p. Reports contents of confidential letter from Michigan about a Mr. Florer, who apparently is being considered for position in School of Education, University of Chicago.

74. To Harper, May 30, 1901. Typed. 2pp. Feels that it is "indispensable" that provision for secondary work be made in planning new Education building.

75. To Harper, June 12, 1901. Typed. 1p. Suggests that in place of an assembly hall and gymnasium, shops and laboratories for secondary school work be provided in the new building.

76. To Harper, July 22, 1901. Written. 2pp. Apologizes for having appointed Mrs. Dewey principal of the Dewey School without having first consulted Harper.

77. To Harper, Sept. 16, 1901. Written. 2pp. "I shall not stand by and see an educational enterprise [Dewey School] with which my name and professional reputation are bound up put at a factitious disadvantage"—by the Parker people.

78. To Wilbur S. Jackman, dean, School of Education, Sept. 26, 1901. Typed "Copy." 4pp. Lists the actions of the School of Education people to which he takes exception.

79. To Harper, Sept. 28, 1901. Written. 1p. Encloses copy of his letter to Jackman. [See preceding item.]

80. To Harper, Oct. 10, 1901. Written. 1p. Has received from R. R. Whitehead a gift of $100 for Dewey School.

81. To Harper, Nov. 8, 1901. Typed. 2pp. Says only nine children are receiving free tuition in Dewey School, and seven of these are children of teachers in the school.

82. To Harper, no date [but written in Jan. 1902]. Written. 1p. Believes Miss K. Allison Welch's work in Dewey School was equivalent to professional training required for teacher certification in New York State.

83. To Harper, Jan. 10, 1902. Typed. 1p. Harper has not informed him of "fundamental plans and conditions" regarding the secondary school part of the School of Education; he [Dewey] is mentally so constituted that he cannot "work in the dark."

84. To Harper, Jan. 29, 1902. Typed. 1p. Best to pay Miss Luanna Robertson, dean of women, South Side Academy, the $300.

85. To Harper, March 3, 1902. Written. 1p. Has filled out teacher certification blank for Miss Welch.

86. To Mrs. Blaine, May 21, 1902. Written. 1p. Thanks her and trustees of Chicago Institute for nominating him as director of university's School of Education.

87. To Mrs. Blaine, June 5, 1902. Written. 1p. Expresses appreciation of motive, spirit, and heartiness of communication from institute trustees.

88. To Alonzo K. Parker, recorder, University of Chicago, July 25, 1902. Mimeographed copy. 8pp. Gives reasons for voting against a proposition to separate men and women students for instruction in the junior colleges of the university.

89. To Mrs. Blaine, Aug. 4, 1902. Written. 1p. Willing to have his name associated with Francis W. Parker School; his relations with staff of university's School of Education have been "most pleasant."

90. To Harper, Oct. 18, 1902. Typed. 1p. Letters of inquiry to Harper's office about courses of School of Education might be sent to Dewey, who would have the appropriate instructor reply.

91. To Francis W. Shepardson, secretary to Harper, Oct. 18, 1902. Typed. Copy. 1p. Is preparing a circular for the School of Education.

92. To Harper, Oct. 25, 1902. Typed. 3pp. Was not possible to get out a School of Education circular by fall because of confusion and inadequacies in planning of special courses.

93. To Harper, Nov. 7, 1902. Typed. 2pp. Defends his inviting members of Dewey School faculty to contribute to decennial volumes articles interpreting results of experience gained in Dewey School.

94. To Shepardson, Nov. 19, 1902. Typed. 1p. Listing of faculty in the bulletin of the School of Education probably should follow that of last May's *Record*.

95. To Harper, Dec. 8, 1902. Typed. 1p. What should he do with Col. Parker's files of letters, etc.?

96. To Harper, Dec. 8, 1902. Typed. 2 pp. A new question has come up—the organization of the School of Education library and its relation to the University Library.

97. To Mrs. Blaine, Jan. 26, 1903. Typed. 2pp. Teachers would like to name University Elementary School for Col. Parker; would this cause confusion with Francis W. Parker School on north side?

98. To Harper, Jan. 27, 1903. Typed. 1p. Is in favor of giving Jackman time to visit normal schools as first step toward working out an accredited list.

99. To Jackman, Feb. 21, 1903. Typed. Copy. 1p. Who without his authorization placed his name on announcement of a Parents' Association meeting? Let it not occur again.

100. To Mrs. Blaine, Feb. 28, 1903. Written. 1p. Sorry to have missed seeing her at the university's Washington celebration.

101 To Harper, April 8, 1903. Typed. 1p. Stanley McCormick, Chicago, has given two maps to the School of Education.

102. To Mrs. Blaine, April 30, 1903. Typed. 2pp. Despite what she has been told, he did secure agreement from two members of Parker School faculty before he recommended combining Dewey School and University Elementary School.

103. To Mrs. Blaine, April 30, 1903. Typed. 1p. Does not believe report that she [Mrs. Blaine] opposed combining Dewey School and University Elementary School if Mrs. Dewey were to be principal.

104. To Harper, no date [probably June, 1903]. Written. 1p. Recommends Mrs. Dewey's appointment as instructor for three years; she already has an appointment as principal for 1903-04.

105. To Harper, June 23, 1903. Telegram. Suggests E. F. Kemp as instructor for summer quarter.

106. To Mary Reed, Aug. 25, 1903. Typed. 1p. Cannot recall why her appointment as associate teacher in the Elementary School was for two years instead of three.

107. To Mrs. Blaine, Oct. 4 [1903]. Written. 1p. Hopes she can visit school and new building.

108. To Harper, Oct. 5, 1903. Typed 1p. There must be $3,000-$4,000 more available for purchase of apparatus and equipment for the School of Education.

109. To Harper, Oct. 9, 1903. Typed. 2pp. German department wants teachers' course in German given through the College of Education.

110. To Harper, Oct. 14, 1903. Typed. 1p. Authorized Angell to offer John B. Watson $1,000 salary to serve as assistant in experimental psychology.

111. To Harper, Oct. 14, 1903. Typed. 3pp. Lists items on which he expects to spend $5,000 of the $6,000 balance in the budget of the School of Education.

112. To Harper, Oct. 16, 1903. Typed. 1p. Present Course Book for the College of Education fails to fulfill purposes for which it was intended.

113. To Jackman, Oct. 16, 1903. Typed. Carbon copy. 5pp. [Harper's name stamped at end, but internal evidence indicates that Dewey is the writer.] Criticizes College of Education Course Book.

114. To Harper, Oct. 24, 1903. Typed. 1p. Asks for

reservation of eastern part of Scammons grounds for use of School of Education.

115. To Harper, Oct. 26, 1903. Typed. 1p. Recommends Alice F. Pitkin as instructor in physical education in the School of Education.

116. To Harper, Oct. 30, 1903. Typed. 1p. Recommends certain members of the faculty of other departments as representatives to serve on the general committee of the College of Education.

117. To Harper, Nov. 3, 1903. Typed. 1p. Answers Harper's criticism that he [Dewey] may have been depriving Dean Jackman "of a sufficiently wide scope of influence."

118. To Harper, Nov. 14, 1903. Typed. 1p. Asks what disposition has been made regarding the supplementary budget.

119. To Harper, Nov. 14, 1903. Typed. 1p. Would be grateful for any assistance Harper can give to a request to the Carnegie Institution from the Association of American College Teachers of Education for funds for research.

120. To Harper, Nov. 18, 1903. Typed. 2pp. As the Laboratory School wound up its career with a credit of $475.46, cannot this be shown on financial statements to the trustees instead of just the deficit for 1902-03?

121. To Jackman, Nov. 18, 1903. Typed. Copy. 5pp. Criticizes Jackman's handling of preparation of Course Book of College of Education.

122. To Harper, Nov. 18, 1903. Typed. 2pp. Criticizes omissions, particularly those relative to credit for practice work, in the Course Book of the College of Education.

123. To Harper, Nov. 18, 1903. Typed. 1p. Asks for information about the Equipment Fund of the School of Education.

124. To Harper, Nov. 19, 1903. Typed. 1p. Asks whether the university has or can make available the services of a private detective.

125. To Harper, Nov. 19, 1903. Typed. 1p. Will call for creation of a standing committee for physical culture and athletics at next meeting of the School of Education faculty.

126. To Harper, Dec. 2, 1903. Typed. 1p. Recommends that Michael Sadler and William Rein be engaged to give courses or lectures next summer.

127. To Harper, Dec. 11, 1903. Typed 2pp. Meant no criticism of the auditor, but still thinks financial statement to trustees should show that Laboratory School had credit instead of deficit.

128. To Harper, Dec. 22, 1903. Typed. 1p. Recommends that Bergson, Windelband, Erdmann, and Ebbinghaus be invited to give "open" lectures next summer.

129. To Harper, Jan. 20, 1904. Typed. 1p. Recommends May Hinman to give assistance in gymnasium work in Elementary School.

130. To Harper, Jan. 21, 1904. Typed 1p. Would be glad to have Harper attend meeting at which training for high-school teachers will be discussed.

131. To Harper, Jan. 29, 1904. Typed. 1p. Wishes instructions as to part of budget against which requisitions are to be drawn.

132. To Harper, Feb. 6, 1904. Typed. 2pp. Recommends that O. Salomon, head of sloyd work in Sweden, be engaged to offer courses in the School of Education in autumn.

133. To Mrs. Blaine, Feb. 8, 1904. Typed. 1p. Thanks her and Flora Cooke, principal of Francis W. Parker School, for work they did on his manuscript ["Education, Direct and Indirect," probably].

134. To Harper, Feb. 12, 1904. Typed 5pp Answers Harper's criticisms of School of Education budget for 1904-05.

135. To Mrs. Blaine, Feb. 24, 1904. Typed. 1p. Hopes she will be able to attend formal opening [of School of Education building].

136. To Harper, April 11, 1904. Typed. 1p. "Other circumstances" will decide the question of whether he will give extension lectures for the university next year.

137. To Harper, April 19, 1904. Typed. 2pp. Considers falling off of High School tuitions result of defects in building facilities.

138. To Harper, April 27, 1904. Typed. 1p. Understands that Harper has facts and considerations important for him [Dewey] to know; asks for interview today.

139. To Mrs. Blaine, April 30 [1904]. Written. 1p. Acknowledges receipt of her letter of April 28.

140. To Harper, May 10, 1904. Typed. 1p. Requests Harper to make clear to trustees that Harper's refusal to reappoint Mrs. Dewey as principal is not cause of his resignation.

141. To Mrs. Blaine, May 12, 1904. Written. 1p. Matters referred to in her letter may be considered better in a personal meeting at her convenience.

142. To Mrs. Blaine, June 11, 1904. Written. 1p. Will be glad to call on her at any time for the conversation she wishes.

143. To Mrs. Blaine, June 16 [1904]. Written. 1p. Will call on her tomorrow afternoon.

[Chicago; no date but obviously
late 1893 or early 1894]

President Harper

Dear Sir:

I desire to submit to you the grounds on which I would most heartily and emphatically urge the consideration of Prof. John Dewey of the University of Michigan for the position of Head-Professor of Philosophy in the University of Chicago.

I. His record and ability as a scholar. He is well known on both sides of the Atlantic for his activity in this respect. Although as yet a young man he has been for nearly ten years one of the most frequent and vigorous contributors to the various philosophical periodicals, and has produced three books, which will be given in full below. After graduation from the Univ. of Vermont in Burlington, Vt., and studying a year there in philosophy under the direction of the President, he took his degree of Ph.D. at the Johns Hopkins University in 1884, and was invited to Michigan by Prof. G. S. Morris who had lectured at Baltimore. After two years he published his Psychology, which at once made him known as an original and acute observer as well as an able thinker. It has been very widely used—at nearly all the Eastern institutions whose professors had not themselves books on the subject, e.g., Bowdoin, Brown, Wellesley, Williams, Smith, etc., and is now in its third edition. In 1888, two years later, he wrote his "Leibniz's New Essays" for the Griggs Series of Philosophical Classics—a book which Prof. Ladd of Yale spoke of in The New Englander as the clearest and most useful of the series. It is more than a clear historical exposition. It shows an insight into the real questions at issue and a mastery of philosophical principles which attest to the maturity of a master, who has a well-thought out basis of his own. In this year he accepted a call to the Professorship of Philosophy in the Univ. of Minn., having two years before been made Asst. Prof. at Michigan. In 1889 on the death of Prof. Morris he was called back to Michigan. Pres. Angell remarked to me, "I don't suppose our students would have allowed us to call any one else." Since then he has published his "Outlines of Ethics," and numerous contributions to

---

[4] This is one of the more interesting items *about* Dewey in the Chicago archives. Mr. McCaul is now calendaring these.

"Mind," "The International Journal of Ethics," "The Monist," "The Philosophical Review," and has been secured as co-editor on the staff of the new Psychological Review. His activity is thus seen to be many sided, in Psychology, History of Philosophy and Ethics, and he has been announced to write a book in the "Library of Philosophy" which will be called "The Principles of Instrumental Logic." This "Library of Philosophy" is a series of very valuable and scholarly books, mainly by English authors.

The above indicates that he is a productive man, one of the most productive, and his work is all of an eminently scholarly character and contains original thought, and contributions to science.

II. He would, I feel confident, be an effective organizer of departmental work. A producer himself, he knows how to guide other men into fruitful lines of research. He is withal a delightful man to work with.

III. As a teacher he is one of the most popular and successful in the Univ. of Michigan. His classes are always large and his students enthusiastic.

IV. As a man he is simple, modest, utterly devoid of any affectation or self-consciousness, and makes many friends and no enemies. He is a man of religious nature, is a church-member and believes in working with the churches. He is moreover actively interested in practical ethical activity and is a valued friend of the Hull House of this city.

I subjoin a list of the more important publications of Prof. Dewey.[5]

*   *   *

Respectfully submitted
JAMES H. TUFTS
[Assistant Professor of Philosophy
University of Chicago]

---

[5] This list has been omitted.

Brief Biographies
of Contributors

By STANLEY LEHRER

To COMPILE THE BOOK, "John Dewey: Master
Educator," the editors have gathered the research
and impressions of educators concerning Dewey
as a teacher-administrator-philosopher. The following are brief biographical accounts of the
contributors who made this book possible.

M. I. BERGER, born in New York City, Aug. 5, 1928,
is associate professor of education, New York State College for Teachers, Albany, from which he received the
A.B. (1950) and M.A. (1952). Columbia University award-
ed the Ph.D. to him in 1956. His career in education
includes positions as social studies teacher and chairman
of the department, Queensbury Public School System,
Glens Falls, N. Y., and lecturer, College of the City of
New York. He has contributed material to the book,
"Public Education in America" (edited by George Z. F.
Bereday and Luigi Volpicelli, 1958), and to the *Journal
of Educational Research, School and Society, Science,* and
Teachers College Record.

ISAAC B. BERKSON was born in Brooklyn, N. Y., Dec.
23, 1891. He earned his B.A. in 1912 from the College of
the City of New York (now The City College of New
York), where he is serving at present as professor of edu-
cation. Both the M.A. (1914) and the Ph.D. (1919) were
received from Teachers College, Columbia University. He
has held such posts as director of the Hebrew Educational
System of Palestine, 1928-35, and professor of education,
The Dropsie College for Hebrew and Cognate Learning,
Philadelphia, 1946-54. In addition to his four books—
"Theories of Americanization" (1920), "Preface to an
Educational Philosophy" (1940), "Education Faces the
Future" (1943), and "The Ideal and the Community"
(1958)—he has written articles for the *Annals* of the
American Academy of Political and Social Sciences, *Edu-
cational Theory, School and Society, Religious Education,*
and *Jewish Education.*

WILLIAM W. BRICKMAN was born in New York City,
June 30, 1913, and was educated at the College of the

City of New York (B.A., 1934, and M.S. in education, 1935) and New York University (Ph.D., 1938). For nearly 20 years he has taught at N.Y.U., where he now is professor of education. In addition, he is serving as editor of *School and Society*, published by the Society for the Advancement of Education of which he is secretary. He was president of the Comparative Education Society, 1956-59, and has traveled abroad extensively, studying the educational systems of countries in South America, Europe, the Middle East, and the Far East. His trips also have taken him to the U.S.S.R. and other lands behind the Iron Curtain. As a writer he has presented much of his work in the *Educational Forum, American Historical Review, Modern Language Journal,* "Encyclopaedia Britannica," "Collier's Yearbook," and the "Encyclopedia of Educational Research." His books are "Guide to Research in Educational History" (1949), "The Changing Soviet School" (co-editor and co-author with George Z. F. Bereday and Gerald H. Read, 1959), and "John Dewey: Master Educator" (edited with Stanley Lehrer, 1959).

Born in New York City, Dec. 23, 1917, MAXINE GREENE studied at Barnard College, Columbia University (B.A., 1938), and New York University (M.A., 1949, and Ph.D., 1955). Prior to her present position as assistant professor of education, N.Y.U., she was assistant professor of English, New Jersey State Teachers College, Montclair. Major writings have appeared in *School and Society, Educational Theory, The Humanist,* and the *Saturday Review.*

WILLIAM HEARD KILPATRICK, who still freshly recollects his acquaintance with John Dewey, was born in White Plains, Ga., Nov. 20, 1871. He received his A.B. (1891), A.M. (1892), and LL.D. (1926) from Mercer University; the Ph.D. (1912) from Columbia University; and another LL.D. (1938) from Bennington College. Important posts that he has held include teacher and principal, Georgia public schools; professor of mathematics, 1897-1906, and acting president, 1903-05, Mercer University; professor of philosophy of education, Teachers College, Columbia University, 1918-38, from which he retired in 1938 as professor emeritus; president, board of trustees, Bennington College, 1930-38; and president, New York Urban League, 1941-51. Over the years he has completed many books, among which are "The Montessori System Examined" (1914), "Froebel's Kindergarten Principles Critically Examined" (1916), "Source Book in the Philosophy of Education" (1923), "Foundations of Method" (1925), "Education for a Changing Civilization" (1926), "Our Educational Task" (1930), "Education and the Social Crisis" (1932), "The Educational Frontier" (editor and co-author, 1933), "Remaking the Curriculum" (1936), "The Teacher and Society" (editor and co-author, 1937), "Group Education for a Democracy" (1940), "Intercultural Attitudes in the Making" (co-editor and co-author, 1947), and "Philosophy of Education" (1951). Paul Monroe's "Cyclopedia of Education," *Childhood Education, School and Society,* and *Educational Forum* have published his articles.

HAROLD A. LARRABEE, Ichabod Spencer Professor of Philosophy and chairman, department of philosophy, Union College, was born in Melrose, Mass., Aug. 20, 1894. His degrees were earned at Harvard College (A.B. *cum laude,* 1916), Columbia University (M.A., 1918), and Harvard University (Ph.D., 1925). He has been vice-president of the Eastern Division, American Philosophical Association; director of the Editorial Center, U.S.A., of the international *Bibliography of Philosophy;* contributing editor, *The Humanist;* and book editor, *Journal of Philosophy.* In addition to his present position at Union College, he is serving as a member, board of editors, *New England Quarterly,* and president, Alpha of New York, Phi Beta Kappa. His books are as follows: "Reliable Knowledge" (1925), "What Philosophy Is" (1928), "Bentham's Handbook of Political Fallacies" (editor, 1952), "Man: Mind or Matter?" (translator, 1951), "In Quest of a New Ethics" (translator, 1953), and "Sensation Creates Life" (translator, 1960). The last three books were originally written by Charles Mayer, Parisian biochemist. Dr. Larrabee's articles and reviews have appeared in the "Encyclopedia of Social Sciences," "Encyclopedia Americana Annual," "Collier's Encyclopedia," *Journal of Philosophy, Philosophical Review, Ethics, New England Quarterly, School and Society, Harper's Magazine, New York Times Book Review,* and *American Heritage.*

On May 29, 1913, ROBERT L. McCAUL was born in Waltham, Mass. He received his education at Harvard College (A.B., 1935), Harvard Graduate School of Education (Ed.M., 1937), and the University of Chicago (Ph.D., 1953). He has served as an assistant, Harvard Psycho-Educational Clinic, 1936-39; a teacher in the University of Chicago's Laboratory School, 1939-43; an assistant professor of English, University of Chicago, 1946-53; and is currently an assistant professor of education and associate director, the University of Chicago's Center for Teacher Education. His writings have been published in the "Encyclopaedia Britannica," "Mental Measurements Yearbook," *School and Society, Review of Educational Research, Journal of Educational Research, School Review, Elementary School Journal, Journal of Higher Education,* and *Georgia Historical Quarterly.*

ROBERT E. MASON, born in Blissfield, Mich., Dec. 10, 1914, earned his A.B. from Huntington College (1953), A.M. from Indiana University (1937), and Ph.D. from Columbia University (1949). He assumed duties as professor of education at Western Reserve University, 1952-58; chairman of the Philosophy of Education Section, National Society of College Teachers of Education, 1957-58; and president, Ohio Valley Philosophy of Education Society, 1958-59. Since 1958, he has been professor of education at the University of Pittsburgh. His book, "Moral Values and Secular Education," was published in 1950. He has contributed articles to *School and Society, Teachers College Record, Journal of Educational Research, Educational Theory, Progressive Education,* and *Phi Delta Kappan.*

Born in Randolph, Ohio, Oct. 28, 1872, JUNIUS L. MERIAM received his education at Oberlin College (A.B., 1895), Harvard University (A.M., 1902), and Columbia University (Ph.D., 1905). His professional career has included positions as superintendent of schools, Wakeman, Ohio, 1895-97, and supervisor of teaching, New York State Normal College, 1899-1901. He taught at the University of Missouri for 20 years and at the University of California, Los Angeles, for 19 years, retiring from U.C.L.A. in 1943 as professor emeritus of education. His writings in educational periodicals number about 60 articles.

Related Writings

From
The Macmillan Company
Horizon Press
University of Chicago Press
Harper & Brothers

The John Dewey Lectureship Series

1959

John Dewey's Challenge to Education

By OSCAR HANDLIN, Professor of History, Harvard University

A Pulitzer Prize winning historian analyzes the American school and its cultural context at the beginning of John Dewey's career. These observations clarify the significance of Dewey's achievement and measure the man against his time with remarkable skill. $2.50

1958

The Climate of Learning

By ORDWAY TEAD, Formerly Chairman of the Board of Higher Education, New York City

A noted teacher and administrator challenges our colleges to overcome mediocrity and intensify the passion for personal intellectual growth which is the hallmark of quality in education. $2.50

Published by

HARPER & BROTHERS

49 East 33rd Street   **New York 16**